Ordinary to Extraordinary

TERRIFIC TREATMENTS FOR GARMENT SEWING

CREATIVE INSPIRATION, TIPS, AND TECHNIQUES

By Lyla J. Messinger

L.J. Designs

Reno, Nevada
A Sew'n Tell Studio book

I dedicate this book, with much love, to my parents Jean and Lyle.
You have always encouraged and supported me in my creative endeavors, without question.
You've given love unconditionally. I return it twofold.

Printed in Canada by Friesens Corporation

A Sew'n Tell Studio book
Editor: Susan Huxley
Cover and Interior Book Designer: Chris Rhoads
Layout Artist: Donna Rossi
Illustrator: John Kocon Illustration
Fashion Photographer: J.P. Hamel Photography
Product Photographer: Robert Gerheart

L. J. Designs, P.O. Box 18923, Reno, NV 89511-0863

ISBN 0-9707893-0-0

L.J. Designs

Meet the Author

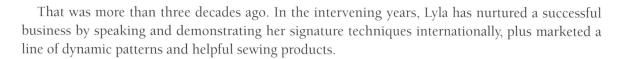

Lyla Messinger was destined to work with textiles. Despite a brief foray into computers, her life has been a full-throttle pursuit of creative sewing.

An avid sewer at a very young age, she channeled her creative energy into a Masters degree in clothing and textiles at the University of Nevada.

That was more than three decades ago. In the intervening years, Lyla has nurtured a successful business by speaking and demonstrating her signature techniques internationally, plus marketed a line of dynamic patterns and helpful sewing products.

The first stop in her sewing "apprenticeship" was the University of Washington, for a Bachelor of Arts degree. Like most starving students, Lyla had a part-time job in her chosen field: a garment inspector for a skiwear manufacturer. It wasn't long, however, before she convinced management to let her work on the machines. Even then Lyla could sew at record speed, so she was allowed to tackle many jobs.

Her formal schooling complete, for a decade Lyla taught math and home economics. These subjects are a perfect match, she believes, because both involve problem solving and numbers. When burnout was imminent, Lyla left the classroom to open a sewing machine and fabric store.

This is where an awareness of her true calling emerged. Lyla liked teaching sewing techniques. She enjoyed exploring all the features on the machines and accessories in her shop. But, more than anything else, she loved the challenge of combining the stitches, threads, machine features, and notions in a tasteful manner to create boutique-quality clothing.

Seven years later, the creative itch was so overpowering that Lyla sold the business to invest all her time in designing clothes, creating techniques, and teaching sewing. She never looked back.

She started her pattern line, L. J. Designs, to offer sewing enthusiasts stylish but simple clothing as canvases for beautiful fabric and the techniques she loves to develop. Through her presentations at the American Sewing Guild annual convention and chapter events, consumer sewing shows, and stores, she continues to share ideas and inspire people to try new techniques.

Contents

On the Edge   70

Bias Without Boundaries   92

Introduction

Sewers are dreamers. Seeing or touching a piece of fabric inspires visions of a wonderful new garment. A spool of decorative thread or interesting tool launches exciting new technique possibilities. We're always looking for ways to turn the ordinary—be it a simple pattern or fabric—into something extraordinary.

This book is a homage to making dreams come true. In these pages you'll find techniques that show you how to create a wardrobe of boutique-quality garments with only a little effort. You can:

- manipulate a humdrum fabric into unique yardage,
- build exciting accent pieces for a garment,
- use a new notion for interesting effects, and
- learn innovative ways to assemble garment pieces.

I'll also explain the inspiration that led to many of the features in "Ordinary to Extraordinary: Terrific Treatments for Garment Sewing." It's my hope that these anecdotes will give you ideas for jump-starting your creativity.

For years students and supporters have asked me to compile my techniques. This book is my way of thanking them for sharing with me. It's wonderful watching them make an idea their own so that the results create a personal style. I really love seeing the sparkle in their eyes as an idea unfolds. The sharing and caring is what makes it all worthwhile. I hope that the "Inspiration Point" tips throughout this book will continue this spirit of creative exploration by showing you fun ways to play with a favorite technique.

In addition, there are more than a hundred color photographs of garments that show you how to apply a technique to a garment. Take a moment to examine the garment "canvas" underneath the surface effects. It's best to choose patterns with simple lines to showcase your work. To make picking a pattern easier for you, most of the photos show garments from L. J. Designs, with the pattern name listed nearby. (Pages 118–119 have ordering information.)

Other photos in this book show you some of my favorite tools, accompanied by instructions on using them. These "Lyla's Notions" features show ways to make your sewing easier. The gathering foot, for example, was designed to ruffle a length of fabric and attach it to a flat piece in a single step. Instead, I used the foot to texture fabric for an accent piece on a shirt, as shown on page 58. I was so excited by the results—and it was so easy to develop—that I explored ways to combine a gathering effect with corded pintucks. (See page 66.) I love this type of problem solving, but I'm always eager to get on to the next challenge.

Thinking that you may feel the same way, the instructions in this book are set up so that you don't have to read the book from cover to cover (unless you want to). Instead, you'll be able to start right in on your favorite technique. The settings provided in the techniques are general. I encourage you to experiment with them so that the finished effect pleases you.

Also with each technique, you'll find a list of supplies needed to recreate the featured effect. I haven't included items that are usually found in most sewing rooms. When a technique is suitable for only specific fabric types, I alert you to this limitation with a Suitable Fabrics entry.

I thought that you might benefit from some of the questions my students ask, so I also included their queries—and my responses—in a FAQ (Frequently Asked Question) in numerous techniques.

Over a decade ago, I opened a sewing store and quickly realized that I didn't push my sewing machines to their limits! I wasn't aware of all the new attachments and notions that were available. Now that I design and teach full time, I count on many people and companies to provide me with up-to-date equipment and supplies. Husqvarna Viking Sewing Machine Company loaned me machines, accessories, and embroidery software. Superior Threads provided threads for garments. The Fasturn Tube Turner came from Crowning Touch, and Clotilde, Inc. supplied the Perfect Pleater, stiletto, and fusible thread shown in the applicable Lyla's Notion features.

I hope you enjoy the creative inspiration in this book as much as I have enjoyed using, developing, and refining the featured techniques I share here with you.

Lyla

Freedom Wrap

Ultimate Broomstick Skirt

SophistiCoat

Function Meets Fashion

Problem solving is one of the more satisfying aspects of sewing. You see an intriguing garment in a boutique, and then set out to duplicate the effect. Finding a way to use a troublesome fabric becomes a quest. A new thread begs for a technique that showcases its beauty. You wonder if there are other ways to use a fun notion in your tool kit.

I'm always in search of a technique that may be the solution to a problem I encountered during construction. Not only do I want to resolve the trouble, but I want the solution to yield a garment that looks like it's a ready-to-wear item from a boutique. I wouldn't wear a garment if someone told me that it looked homemade.

While solving some of the problems that cropped up during the construction of garments over the years, I discovered that the solutions can also be used as decorative detailing on other pieces. Resolving a fitting problem on the back waist of a vest led to texturizing a larger piece of fabric. (See page 44). A functional bias tube, used as a button loop, became a more creative closure. (See page 10.) The key is to open your eyes to specific places for creating fashionable details. And that's what this chapter is about: learning to take purely functional techniques to the next level.

Breaking the Rules

*L*et's pretend we're rebellious teenagers. If a book tells you that a sewing process must be done a certain way, ask "why," and experiment. I do this all the time. My sewing machines still work, my house is still standing, and the sewing police haven't hauled me off to prison. Most importantly, I had fun.

My Freedom Wrap, shown at lower right, can be worn several ways. The hem edge needs a nice finish on the right and wrong sides.

I made the hem on my first Freedom Wrap by stitching ¼ inch from the raw edge, pressing a narrow hem to the wrong side twice, and then stitching it in place. This gave the look I was after, but it took me over an hour just to press the edge to prepare it for stitching because the hem is so long. That method is for the birds.

I had to break a sewing rule to find a technique that's faster and looks great. The solution turned out to be making the final row of stitching with the right side down, so that the bobbin thread ends up on the outside of the garment. Until I came up with this idea, I had it in my head that whenever I top-stitched I should do it from the right side. Why are we taught to topstitch from the right side? The bottom of a stitch, made by the bobbin thread, isn't as pretty as the upper side because of the way the stitch is formed on a machine. Bobbin thread stitching doesn't look as bad as we think. No one has ever grabbed the hem of a Freedom Wrap to see which side has the prettiest stitches.

There's another advantage to this approach: Stitching the final row wrong side up, with decora-

tive thread in the bobbin, I can ensure that the inner edge is always caught in the stitching.

Decorative thread can really jazz up an edge, so I frequently use it for bobbin-stitched hems. Besides, if I'm breaking a rule, I want everyone to know that I'm aware that I'm doing it. Beautiful thread always draws attention.

Freedom Wrap

I try to make the construction process for the garments in my pattern collection as simple and quick as possible. A standard narrow hem took too long to make on the L-O-N-G edge of this wrap, so a new technique had to be found. I developed an edge finish that requires no pins, no pressing, and looks decorative when complete. (See page 3.)

Bobbin-Stitching a Quick Hem

Simple steps for hemming a long edge yield fast, attractive, and reversible results. The topstitching is a straight stitch, but, with lightweight threads, you might also try a triple straight stitch for a more pronounced look.

Versa Jacket and Asymmetrical Skirt

Comfortable with using decorative thread for a bobbin-stitched hem, I graduated to regular sewing thread. This technique is great for curved hems, scarf edges, and one-layer collars.

1. Set up a balanced 3-thread overlock, and adjust the stitch width as desired. The stitch width determines the width of the finished hem. For a narrower hem, use your right needle and a narrow setting. For a wider hem, use your left needle and a wider stitch. Use regular, matching, serger thread. Always make a test sample. If you don't have a serger, sew ¼ inch from the raw fabric edge using a very narrow zigzag stitch (3 length, 1 width).

2. Serge or zigzag the raw hem edge.

3. Place regular or decorative thread in the bobbin on a sewing machine. The thread can be any weight. Use regular thread in the needle. Don't hesitate to play with the tension. An unbalanced stitch is often more interesting because both the bobbin and top thread show on one side.

4. Position the garment on the machine bed with the wrong side up. Using the serger stitching as a turning guide, fold the first several inches of the serged edge to the wrong side of the fabric. Don't sew yet.

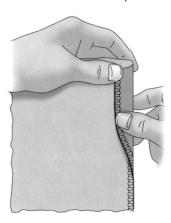

5. Fold the serged edge to the wrong side again, to hide the serging. Don't press or pin the edge because you're only working on a few inches of the hem. If you pull slightly on the edge the serger stitching turns the edge. Pull on a few inches at a time to prevent the curve from straightening.

6. Edge stitch along the fabric fold, from the wrong side of the garment, using a stitch length of 3 to 4 mm. Continue double folding and pulling the edge as you proceed.

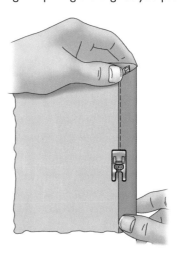

7. Press the hem edge up to, and including, the stitching.

SophistiCoat

The 3-thread overlocking on this coat isn't on the edge. Well, it is now, but it didn't start that way. It's ⅝ inch from the original raw edge. The serger stitching with Pearl Crown Rayon thread looks great because a cutting guide and stable edge were established by basting with water-soluble thread ⅝ inch from the raw edge.

I often fall in love with a fabric without considering how difficult it will be to sew. After all, figuring out easy ways to work with the yardage is part of the fun. But I struggled when I turned a stretchy knit fabric into a sample garment.

As I worked on the hem, the edge grew longer and longer. It wasn't going to lay flat as intended, despite my

The technique name, Bobbin-Stitched Hem, has stuck, even though you can also use a serger chain stitch. Just change stitches, place decorative thread in the looper, and follow the step-by-step bobbin-stitching instructions. (See page 3.)

efforts to control the stretch by scrunching the fabric behind the presser foot as I stitched (called Ease Plus).

Turning to my supply of notions, I realized that using Ultra-Soft Double-Sided Fusible in an unconventional manner might be the solution. It was. The finished hem was flat and the fusible, tucked inside the hem allowance, was invisible because it stretched with the fabric. See Controlled Knit Hem on page 5.

The ultimate sewing sin is tossing out a fabric because it isn't attractive. Your stash diminishes and an opportunity to stretch your creativity is lost.

I purchased a plaid silky for a texturizing experiment. I thought the colors would block nicely. The results weren't great, so the fabric went into a closet. On another shopping expedition, I bought a fascinating fabric that had holes in it. I had no idea what to do with it. It, too, went into a closet. One day, when I opened the closet, I discovered that these two fabrics had made friends. I couldn't bear to break them up, so I put them together to create a new fabric with beautiful drape. I like the results much more than either one by itself.

Zea Vest Collection

There is hope for ugly fabric. Certainly, it can be relegated to testing the fit of new patterns. But why not use it to make a garment, like my Ugly Fabric Vest? The offending fabric barely peeks out between the holes in the overlay.

Boutique Technique

Controlled Knit Hem

While it's tempting to merely fuse a hem allowance in position, your best bet is stitching stretchy knits. Ultra-Soft Double-Sided Fusible (UsDsF) keeps the task from turning into a nightmare.

1. Finish the hem edge with 3-thread overlocking. You can also clean finish it by straight stitching ¼ inch from the edge, pressing the fabric to the wrong side along the stitching, and then edge stitching the folded fabric in position.

2. Press UsDsF, paper side up, ¼ inch from the hem edge on the wrong side of the fabric. Use the inner edge of the serger stitching or clean finish as a guide for even, accurate placement of the UsDsF strip along the fabric. Pull the paper off the UsDsF.

3. Fold and pin the hem allowance to the wrong side. Press the hem allowance, keeping the iron ¼ inch away from the serged edge and removing the pins as you work. This allows you to press the hem without creating an unsightly ridge on the outside of the garment.

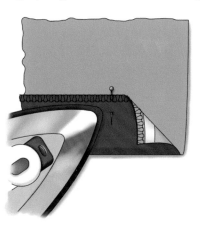

4. Install a stretch double needle 2.5/75 or 4.0/75 on your sewing machine and set the stitch to 3.5- or 4-mm long. Sew with the right side of the garment up, making sure you stitch directly through the UsDsF. You can secure the hem with a serger cover stitch instead of the double needle stitching.

Asymmetrical Tunic & Skirt

The hem on this Slinky Knit dress has always been one of my favorites. The treatment is commonly seen in ready-to-wear. Because the double needle stitching has built-in give, it works beautifully on knit fabrics. A strip of flexible, double-sided fusible webbing controls the fabric's stretch.

Understanding Necessity and Invention

Many times having a product on hand inspires me to try something new. That's why I'm sharing some of my favorite notions and ideas with you in this book. Hopefully, you will use the information to lead you places you never dreamed of going!

Did you ever search in vain for the perfect ribbing to apply to a special garment, and give up in frustration? My memory is still too fresh.

I was making a pieced jacket from cotton woven fabrics. My inspiration was a jacket by a well-known design team, which consisted of pieced printed and solid fabrics. To create printed fabrics, I used various machine techniques on a solid piece of fabric. The ribbing had to match the jacket fabric but sweatshirt ribbing would have looked ridiculous. Then it dawned on me that Stitch'n Stretch Elastic would do the trick.

I first used Stitch'n Stretch Elastic for a vest. The garment started with ties to cinch the back waist for a better fit. Upon wearing the vest, I discovered that the knotted ties felt awful when I leaned against a chair back. In my quest for a pattern line of comfortable clothes, I replaced the tie with a piece of Stitch'n Stretch Elastic at the dip in the lower back.

You can do the same with any vest. Sew or baste the shoulder seams and put on the vest. Mark a placement line at the desired position for the elastic. Cut a 9-inch long piece of elastic. Attach the elastic fol-lowing the instructions on page 46. These steps are part of Stitch'n Stretch Elastic Texturizing, which is another technique that uses the product.

Cut a Stitch'n Stretch ribbed cuff from a separate fabric piece. Serge the bottom edge. Place the elastic on the wrong side with the lowest edge above the serging. With water-soluble thread, baste the elastic to the sleeve cuff along the marked lines. Fold the elastic to the wrong side and straight stitch along the basting. Draw in the elastic cords.

Boutique Technique

Pleating a Godet

Making pleats is as simple as pushing fabric into slots in the Perfect Pleater, setting them with heat and a Rajah Press Cloth. The cloth releases a chemical that permanently sets the pleats.

1. Decide if you want soft or precise pleats. Place the Perfect Pleater on your ironing board, right side up.

2. Select an accent fabric that's at least 50% polyester. Place an edge of the fabric at one end of the pleater, right side down, and use a credit card to push fabric into the first slot. Continue pushing fabric into the slots until you fill the Perfect Pleater or have enough pleats for the pattern piece. Work slowly and precisely for controlled pleats, or quickly and not so precisely for a more random look.

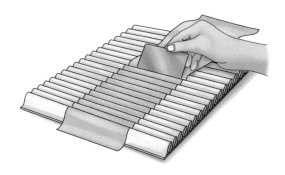

3. Place a Rajah press cloth on top of the pleats, and press. The heat and steam of the iron releases chemicals into the fabric. Let the fabric cool completely.

4. Press basting tape or a strip of double sided fusible along both edges of the pleats before removing the fabric from the pleater.

5. Cut out the pattern piece. Baste the pleats, if desired. If one edge of the pleats will be hemmed, do so now. I like

Kanisha

A splash of interest where it's least expected adds to a garment's appeal. Adding a plain sheer panel to this medium-weight linen wouldn't look right. Pleating the fabric gave it enough visual texture to balance the weight of the main fabric.

using a rolled hem on fine pleated fabric. Stitching a hem after the fabric is pleated makes it flare at the bottom. For a controlled hem, stitch the hem in the fabric first, and then pleat it.

6. Sew the pleated piece into the garment.

Once I have a notion or piece of equipment around, I often think of other uses for it. It may be purchased for the manufacturer's intended use, but I end up doing something totally different with it. I may be playing with a particular technique, and see or think of a piece of equipment. Somehow, that item just jumps on board and moves into my current project.

One example of being inspired by a piece of equipment is the use of pleated fabric for a garment detail. Piping added nice detail along the front edge and collar of a dress. However, I was looking for a way to add more interest. The same fabric was too light for many applications but, when pleated, worked perfectly as godets inserted in the side seams.

Avoiding Narrow Minded Thinking

Many times we look at something from a very narrow perspective. If it was developed for a certain task, that's all it's used for. But this leaves so many unexplored possibilities. Consider different ways that you can use a notion and apply a stitching detail in an entirely new way.

A gathering presser foot was designed to gather a ruffle and attach it to a flat piece of fabric all in one step. But, if you think about how it works and about other garment pieces you may want to gather, you may figure out a way that the gathering foot can help. Several techniques in this book take advantage of the gathering foot's function, but you won't see a ruffle anywhere. Gathered Piping, Gathered Pintucks and Gathered Texture starting on pages 85, 66, and 58, respectively, all show you innovative ways to make more boutique-quality garments.

What does a food grater do? If you only thought about finely slicing cheese, carrots or cabbage, you're missing some fun texturizing experiments. (See page 55.)

Does thinking of pintucking automatically remind you of christening gowns and romantic heirloom garments? That's what I thought. Pintucks didn't impress me because frilly isn't my style. Pushing through this barrier, I explored using pintucks to define printed areas on fabric. I then expanded my repertoire by creating pintucked fabric accents. See Random Corded Pintucks on page 61.

There was a time when decorative stitching was relegated to children's clothing. A machine with all sorts of decorative stitches spurred me into using the features for accents on my garments. Over the years, I pushed myself to use them more and more. Upon acquiring another new machine, with yet more decorative stitches, I tried them all out on a single piece of fabric, which I then turned into a jacket lapel. (See page 16.)

Expand your creativity a bit at a time. Look at one notion or tool. Think how you used it, or how it was intended to be used. Now try to think of just one other thing you could do with it to make your sewing easier, create a new accent, or allow you to just have fun.

Also try pushing yourself to try fabrics that you don't ordinarily use. Fabric that ravels easily is one that many of us avoid. Me, too. Yet I wasn't able to control my fabric-holic tendencies when I found a beautiful hand-woven piece at a sewing show.

Then came the challenge. Rather than fighting the raveling, I decided to turn it to my advantage. I fringed crosswise edges of strips and applied them to the surface of the garment. (See page 75.)

Polar Fleece can also offer construction and design challenges. I started working with it when I was developing my SophistiCoat pattern. It turns out to be the perfect style for this popular fleece, which looks great, is comfortable to wear, and is easy to sew.

The only obstacle was topstitching the pocket. The finished stitching looked bad because the stitches sank in the plush fabric surface. The fabric puffed out unevenly over the stitching. I had to move beyond the concept that topstitching must be straight stitches in fabric.

Boutique Technique

Topstitching with Cord

Select a cord, Pearl Crown Rayon for example. It should be the color that you want for the topstitching.

1. Install a cording foot on your machine. Thread the cord through the hole in the presser foot. This guides the cord as you sew. If you don't have a cording foot, place the cord on the fabric, and keep it aligned with the needle and the center of the presser foot.

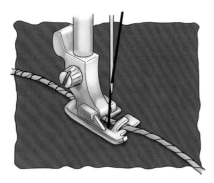

2. Thread the machine with regular sewing thread that matches the fleece.

3. Choose a stitch. It needs to swing left and right, move forward and repeat. A hand appliqué or blanket stitch works well. When stitched out, it looks like a series of backward, stacked capital Es. Adjust the stitch length to at least 4. Adjust the width to a narrow setting (about 1 to 1½), so that the stitch is just wide enough to easily cover the cord.

4. Stitch over the cord. The matching thread disappears into the plush fabric. Where it crosses the contrast color cord, it pushes it into the fleece, giving the appearance of a stitch.

Heavy cording, chosen to match the color of the garment shown at left, solved my topstitching dilemma. Instead of trying to stitch with that heavy thread, I couched it to the fleece. The effect is similar to topstitching.

LaConner Jacket

Making Creative Closures

*B*uttons and buttonhole treatments constantly inspire me to break traditional barriers. Why use a plain closure when there are so many creative options? With very little effort you can give your garment an entirely unique personality.

Consider a shirt with five button closures evenly spaced down center front. Now visualize the same shirt with 10 buttons, grouped in pairs. What an interesting look. Now push a little further, and change the buttonholes to loops. They could be inserted into a seam or be part of a couched design on the shirt front.

A loop solves many problems that an odd-shaped or large button causes. Rather than a large buttonhole, the eye focuses on the interesting closure.

I frequently use loop closures because I am known to look for closures in odd places. Antique stores are great sources for old buttons and buckles, for example, as are accessory and department stores. Pendants and earrings, with a little structural change, look great on garments.

A button, bead or bauble often inspires my garment closures. The color or design worked perfectly with a fabric but the size, shape or way that the "button" attached to the fabric was a challenge.

Several years ago, I visited an antique button store in New Orleans. The elderly proprietor was an absolute delight. She had a story to tell about the history of every button in the place. One of the buttons I couldn't resist was a hand-hammered brass button, with "Paris" stamped on the back. The storeowner told me that the factory that produced these buttons closed in 1890.

The beautiful tones in the button's surface went perfectly with a mohair fabric that I wanted to use to make a coat. Since I only had one button, I wanted to make it an integral part of the closure design. I simply created a length of fabric-covered cord, formed it into a pleasing freeform design, and couched it in place on the finished coat. The button loop is part of the design, which is there only as a decoration.

A treasured antique button takes center stage. The piece is framed by a motif that extends into a loop that substitutes for a buttonhole. Hate making buttonholes? Then a corded closure is a great solution. I almost always use a loop when working on hand-made or loosely woven fabrics. It places less stress on the fabric than a buttonhole.

I attached the cord with invisible thread, a one-toe zipper foot, and the blind hemstitch. The cord rolled up over the stitching so it looks like it was hand-stitched to the coat. If your machine has a two-toe zipper presser foot, you can't use it to couch the cord. It can be hand stitched instead. Did I say that? Let me revise that comment: it can be couched by hand *if* you like to hand sew.

The variety of looks made possible by couching yarns or cords on a fabric is amazing. Vary the cord, the stitch, and the thread for an unlimited combination of designs.

Students frequently ask me why I often close my garments with loops rather than buttonholes. I prefer loops because they disappear under the button. This puts the attention where it belongs: on the closure. In addition, a large buttonhole looks unattractive coupled with a large or oddly shaped button.

(When I refer to a button, I'm actually talking about a bead, earring, or any other bauble that works. After all, why use a button when there are so many other wonderful objects?)

A Chinese coin languished in my stash for some time until I found fabric that worked well with it. I turned the fabric into a garment using my Lyla's Vest pattern. Again, I only had one closure. This vest has a single button closure and a loop instead of a buttonhole, which is ideal for the large coin.

Serger chain makes a subtle statement when used on the closure for this cozy coat. The technique is the same as the one used to secure the fabric tube loop and ties for the Chinese button.

Fabric tubes aren't the only thing you can use for loops and ties on closures. After finishing the edges of a coat with Success serger yarn and a balanced 3-thread overlock stitch, I stitched a length of thread without fabric under the presser foot. If you try this, gently guide the serger chain behind the presser foot so that it doesn't bunch up on the feed dogs.

I attached the loop ties to the coat the same way that I applied the fabric tubes for the Chinese coin.

Before adding the button, I placed the right (buttonhole) side of the coat in position on top of the stitched cords. To attach the button, first pull the serger chains through the buttonhole. Now draw two chains

Lyla's Vest

How do you sew a coin with a single hole in the center, to a garment? Place the center of two crossed fabric tubes on the closure placement position on the garment front. Bar tack or otherwise stitch them in place. Pull the ends of the tubes through the center hole. Tie knots in the cords until the coin can't fall off, then add beads to the ends of the tubes.

through one hole in the button and two chains through another hole in the button. Here's the technical part: Tie a knot to hold the button in position, and add a few more to the ends of the serger chains. The closure and coat is easily opened. By attaching the button in this manner, a shank is automatically created.

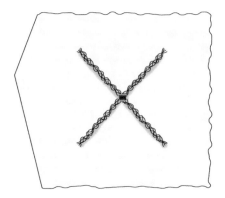

As you can see, this concept is so simple that only your imagination limits the items you can use as your "button" and loop. I even use pierced earrings. If you only need a single closure, there's always a spare. To do the same, just make sure that the top of the earring

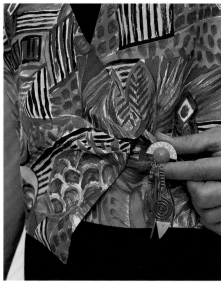

Lyla's Vest

When I made this bright summer vest, I really wanted to find a fruit button for it. I had no luck in that department, so I headed off to my local stores in search of an earring—not to wear with the vest, but to put on it. I bent the post into a u-shaped shank with a pair of needle nose pliers and stitched it to the garment as I would any button with a shank.

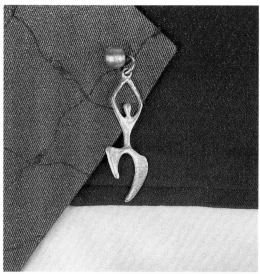

Lyla's Vest

An eye-catching gold man has the whole world in his hands and still manages to keep this vest closed. The closure came from an accessory store. I noticed him in the window, hanging from a leather necklace. I just had to turn him into a vest closure. The only problem I had was the lack of a substantial shape at the top to hold a loop or buttonhole in place. I added the world, which is a round, gold button with a shank, above his hands.

is wide enough to prevent the loop closure from slipping off. My only caution is about cleaning. Depending on the earring's composition, you may have to remove it before washing or dry cleaning the garment.

While in the jewelry department, take a look at the necklaces and other accessories. Keep your eyes open to find some wonderful accent pieces.

A closure merely needs to hold a garment together. Why use a boring button and buttonhole? Loops, earrings, stunning single buttons, and other inventive baubles create a more interesting focal point on a garment. Start picking up unique items as you shop.

Again, I'm going to ask you to think outside the box. We all consider buttons, buttonholes, snaps, and loops as types of closures. But what about belts? In most cases, we don't need them to hold a garment together, but they do buckle, snap, and button closed. My favorite belt is a fabric version that students love to learn to construct. It's special because it only covers the front of the pants and it's designed to hide an elasticized waistband.

There are many times when we want pants and skirts with elastic waistbands, but sacrifice comfort for the tailored look of a fitted waistband. Now you can have the comfort of elastic with this simple idea!

My technique gives the stitched look of a ready-to-wear version. Part of the success is a special product, called Stitch Through Elastic, which stretches to over twice it's original length and recovers after it's stitched.

Boutique Technique

Belting an Elasticized Waistband

Copy the shape of a favorite belt for your new version. One side should be the same shape as the side seam of the pants at the waist in order to attach it to a garment side seam. Shape the other side of the belt into an interesting point or curve. Make sure that the belt is slightly wider than the garment's elastic waistband.

1. Put on your garment and pin a piece of pattern tracing paper on top of the front waistband.

2. Draw a pencil line on the paper to mark the position of the top of the elastic and the side seams. There's no need to trace the bottom and left side of the waistband because they're altered.

3. Remove the tracing paper from your body. Draw a lower edge for the belt, ensuring that it's slightly wider than the garment's waistband. Shape the remaining end. For seam allowances, add ⅝ inch outside all of the lines.

5. Using your new pattern, cut two belt pieces from a co-ordinating or matching fabric. Interface the wrong side of one piece. For knits, interface both pieces.

You can have the look of tailored pants and the comfort of an expandable waistband. Just hide the gathered front with a belt. The fabric is attached to one side seam, covers the front, and then buttons at the opposite side.

6. With right sides together, sew around all edges except the short side that attaches to the side seam.

7. Turn the belt right side out. Fold ⅝ inch of the open end inside the belt, press. Topstitch or decoratively stitch around the edges of the belt. Edge stitch the folded end to the right side seam on the right side of the garment.

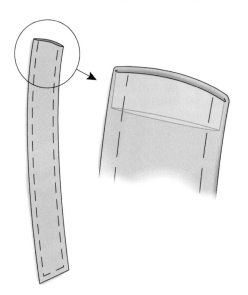

8. Sew a closure, Velcro, fabric ties, or buttonholes near the shaped, loose end of the belt. Attach a corresponding closure to the garment's left side.

LaConner Jacket

Zea Vest Collection

Convertible Jacket

Stitching with Style

This chapter is all about creating your own fabric using little more than leftovers from your stash and the stitches on your machine.

I promise that you'll never look at plain fabric the same way. What was once boring yardage now has tremendous possibilities: cover the surface with stitching, join twisted strips, attach abstract appliqués, or piece it with curved seams. You can even abandon the fabric altogether, and create yardage with little more than tidbits of decorative thread, ribbon, and yarn.

In this chapter you'll find step-by-step guidance on making boutique-quality material and applying machine stitches in exciting new ways.

None of the techniques take long to create and there isn't any excruciating hand stitching. I've used some basic notions and supplies to make the processes as quick and painless as possible. The techniques are easy to master.

Is the lapel fabric from Guatemala? Mexico? Neither, although students have guessed both of these countries and many more. The exotic fabric is from my studio. The piece is a selection of decorative stitches that I applied all over the surface of a base fabric. It's a stress-free technique that works best when you play with your machine and threads.

Stitch Sampler

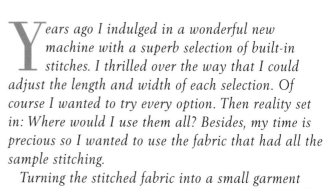

Ultimate Broomstick Skirt

Years ago I indulged in a wonderful new machine with a superb selection of built-in stitches. I thrilled over the way that I could adjust the length and width of each selection. Of course I wanted to try every option. Then reality set in: Where would I use them all? Besides, my time is precious so I wanted to use the fabric that had all the sample stitching.

Turning the stitched fabric into a small garment piece, a lapel in this case, was the solution. I traced the shape of the pattern piece on the fabric and cut it out with very large seam allowances. Then I marked a few places where I should change the direction of my rows of stitching. The excess fabric around the edges let me stitch without worrying that I'd distort the pattern shape if the stitching distorted the fabric.

This project took very little planning. In one pleasant, stress-free sewing session I had my fabric. In no time at all it was worked into the jacket and I was wearing the finished garment. I gained valuable insight into the placement of stitching when people commented on the finished garment. (See the Inspiration Point on page 20.)

Supplies

Bobbin thread

Chalk

Interfacing (optional, depending on fabric weight)

Lightweight machine embroidery thread*

Water-soluble stabilizer

Suitable Fabric

Avoid stretchy knits; nubby, loose weaves; and sheers.

*The appearance of your Stitch Sampler is versatile because it changes drastically whenever you change the stitch selection and the color or type of thread.

Think how much fun it would be to try out all the decorative stitches on a new machine if you could use the results as a lapel, cuff, collar or pocket on a garment—or even as the fabric for piping or trim. You can do just that with these easy steps.

Getting Started

Preparation is simply a matter of setting up the machine and making some basic design decisions. The stitched fabric looks more authentic when the stitching is grouped into sections that occasionally change direction.

1. Using chalk, trace the pattern piece on the fabric background.

2. Interface the back of the fabric, if necessary. Make your interfacing decision the same way that you determine the need for interfacing on the wrong side of any other garment piece.

3. Decide where you plan to change the direction of the stitching. Pretend that you're joining smaller pieces of fabric, as if you're quilting. A pleasing distance is 4 to 6 inches apart. These design lines can be at any angle. On a lapel, I avoid lines that are ex-

actly vertical. Chalk the design lines on the right side of the fabric. If your fabric has a nap, see "Stabilizing the Fabric," on page 18, before drawing the directional lines.

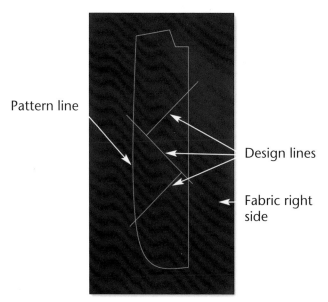

Pattern line

Design lines

Fabric right side

4. Cut the shape from the fabric 1 inch beyond the chalk outline of the pattern piece. It's very important that you leave this extra inch of fabric beyond all the edges of the garment piece. During the stitch application, it's entirely possible that the fabric will draw in a bit. The extra fabric beyond the chalk outline ensures that the finished work will be large enough for the pattern shape.

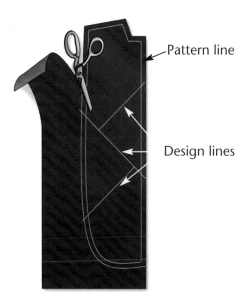

Pattern line

Design lines

Stabilizing the Fabric

Improve the definition of the decorative stitching by stabilizing the fabric.

I prefer using a water-soluble stabilizer, placed on the wrong side of the fabric. For plush or napped fabrics, place the stabilizer on the right side. (Draw the lines for the change of stitching direction on the stabilizer rather than the fabric.) This prevents the stitches from disappearing in the nap.

Making the Satin Stitches

Define the sections on the fabric by satin stitching along the chalk lines.

1. Set the machine for a short (⅓- to 1-mm long) satin stitch and a 2-mm width. Wind bobbin thread on the bobbin. (This very lightweight thread helps draw the needle thread through the fabric.) Play with the settings until you like the stitched results.

2. Loosen the top, or tighten the bobbin, tension until both threads meet on the wrong side of the fabric. Thus adjusted, the satin stitching has smoother edges. If the bobbin case has an extension (finger), run the bobbin thread through this to tighten the tension.

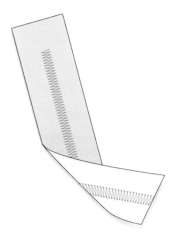

3. Place the stabilizer on the fabric.

4. Using only one color, make one line of satin stitching along all of the chalked lines that block out sections inside the pattern shape. Don't sew the pattern's outline.

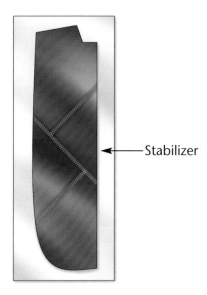

Stabilizer

5. Change the needle thread color as desired and sew additional rows of satin stitching. Use the design lines as guides. Place the edge of the presser foot along the previous line of stitching so that you can work quickly with minimal marking. Work away from the design lines in each section. Continue making rows of satin stitches in this manner until all the outlined design areas are filled.

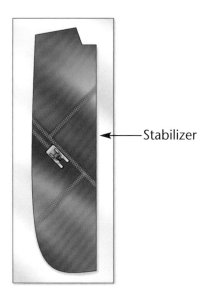

Stabilizer

inspiration point

Cord the satin stitching to give it more dimension. This takes time because the cord at the beginning and end of each row must be pulled to the wrong side of the fabric to finish the piece. (See Step 1 of "Finishing" on page 20.)

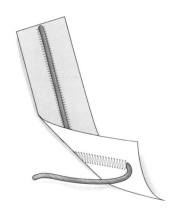

Decorative Stitching

Sew between rows of satin stitching with decorative stitches to create an interesting piece.

Now you're ready to program some stitches or use the preset ones in your machine. Something as simple as the triple straight stitch or zigzag looks interesting with the right thread or color choices. The key is experimenting. Give yourself permission to play.

Stitch combinations look best when you group similar items. For parallel rows in a section, try to select stitches that work together, or are similar in style. For example, sharp edged shapes work well with other geometric stitches. Solid satin stitches aren't as effective when combined with open designs. These aren't steadfast rules. Your personal preferences are more important.

Thread color is a highly personal decision. I just lay out a preliminary selection and pick out the ones I want as I stitch. You can copy color combinations from a finished product: anything from a fabric print, to a painting, or even wallpaper.

Thread type is constant throughout.

Stitch order isn't a big consideration. I don't spend a lot of time deciding what to use for each row. Just pick stitches that you want to try.

Spacing between the rows of decorative stitching is automatic, since each line goes between a pair of satin stitched rows.

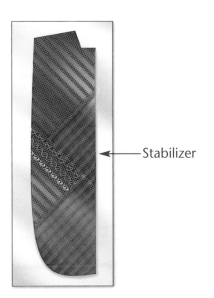

— Stabilizer

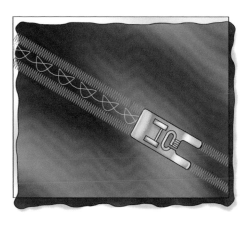

Finishing

The stitched fabric needs very little handling to make it ready for assembly.

1. If you corded any of the stitching, use a hand sewing needle to pull the ends of the cord to the wrong side of the fabric. Knot each cord and cut off the excess. Apply a dab of liquid seam sealer to secure the knot. Make sure the liquid doesn't get on the fabric. Another way to secure the knot is fusing a piece of interfacing or stay tape to the knot.

2. Remove the stabilizer according to the manufacturer's directions.

3. Decorative stitching sometimes distorts the fabric, so cut your pattern piece from the stitched sampler by placing the pattern piece on top. Don't worry about the minimal amount of stitching that unravels at the raw edges, because these will be in the seam allowances of the finished garment.

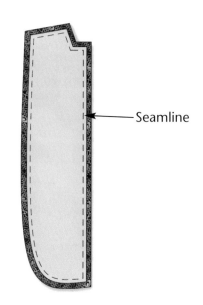

— Seamline

inspiration point

Wearing this jacket at a sewing convention was a learning experience. One person after another asked me about the lapel. People who attend these shows are avid sewers. Why didn't they realize it was an embellished piece? It wasn't obvious because the decorative stitching extended into the seamlines. Often in garments that we sew, embellishments stop short of the seam allowances. It seems that designs only go into seam allowances when a piece is a print or has all-over embroidery. To achieve a boutique-quality look for any garment shape that has all-over embroidery, stitch the fabric before you cut out the pattern piece.

The clean, contemporary look of this appliqué owes its appearance to an unobtrusive application. Heavy satin stitching commonly used to secure appliqué edges was replaced with barely visible machine sewing. Now the design and fabrics are the focal point—not satin-stitched outlines.

Jigsaw Appliqué

LaConner Jacket

I stumbled across this technique when I was looking for a way to secure an appliqué to a garment without making traditional heavy satin stitches around each shape. It was important to downplay the outlines because I wanted the interlocking shapes to take center stage.

But there's a good reason for using satin stitching: it prevents fraying along raw fabric edges of the appliqué shapes. My challenge became finding an alternative.

Because I was working with a woven, I considered the technique used for Shaped Facing on page 25. Once again, I let a notion guide the way to a simple solution. A very fine fusible bias stay tape controls the raveling and eases the application process. Merely apply the tape to the raw edges, turn them under, fuse the shape to the garment, and then use an almost invisible edge stitch for extra security.

The overlapping shapes of a jigsaw design aren't that complex. A portion of one shape sits on another. When you choose your appliqué design, plan on cutting a hole in at least one of the fabric shapes. The hole can be any shape. A portion of a second shape is then inserted into the hole to create an interlocking design.

Supplies

Olfa Rotary Point Cutter

Paper larger than the appliqué design

Sulky KK 2000 Temporary Spray Adhesive

Super Fine Bias Fusible Stay Tape

Wonder Invisible Thread (or matching embroidery)

Wooden iron* (optional)

*A 5- to 6-inch long piece of hardwood with a tapered end, used by quilters to press open ¼-inch wide seam allowances.

Suitable Fabric

The appliqué is any woven fabric and the garment can be made from a woven or non-woven.

Creating a Design

It's possible to work with any shape with the Jigsaw Appliqué technique. Using another design as a launching point is easier than starting from scratch. If you feel so inclined, drawing shapes is a great option as well.

Art deco designs in a travel magazine inspired the shapes on the jacket shown on page 21. Each piece was married with the next as they were applied to the garment. The motif was simplified at seams where the color of the garment pieces changed.

What kind of statement do you want the finished piece to make? Consider a single, small motif as a subtle accent or put shapes together like a jigsaw puzzle.

For inspiration, look at designs in books, magazines, mail order catalogs, wallpaper . . . even the Yellow Pages. Shapes on buildings and in nature can lead to great appliqués. I carry a book and pen in my purse to sketch designs that catch my eye. For a Jigsaw Appliqué, copy or draw shapes that have fairly smooth curves.

As you plan the appliqué position, consider whether you want the work to run over a seam. In this case, you need to plan the appliqué a bit more because it's easier to apply an appliqué while the fabric pieces are still flat. Before attaching the work, assemble the gar-ment pieces until the target seam is finished. Stick with a single shape at this location for continuity and ease of application.

Preparing the Appliqué

Use your design sketches and ideas to make patterns that are suitable for a garment.

1. Trace or sketch the design on paper. If it's too small for the garment, enlarge it on a photocopier.

2. Drawing over your original lines, tweak the design until you're happy with the appearance. Perhaps there is a straight edge that you think might look better as a curve, or a fat section that should be thinned so it doesn't overpower the other shapes?

3. Within the motif, look for shapes that have an opening in them, or create a hole in an existing shape. For example, cut a small triangular hole at one end of a kidney shape and insert a lightning bolt in one side.

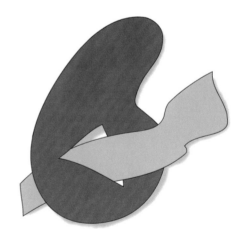

4. To envision how the colors of your appliqué fabrics will look, color the paper shapes.

5. Trace each of the shapes for your design on pattern tracing paper. Draw ¼-inch wide seam allowances around the outer edges. Cut through the paper along the lines to make your patterns.

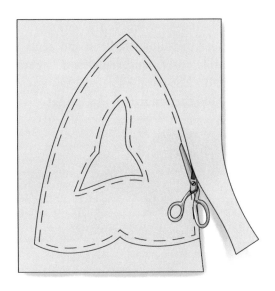

6. Cut the pattern shapes from the appliqué fabrics.

Preparing the Edges

Apply bias tape to the edges of each appliqué shape. The following steps explain the process for one shape. After making it, repeat the process for the remainder.

1. Apply adhesive spray to the non-fusible side of a length of Super Fine Bias Fusible Stay Tape.

FREQUENTLY ASKED QUESTION

How do I keep the force of the spray from flipping the tape?

Hold the can far enough away from the tape to keep it from blowing around and approach the tape directly from above.

2. Finger-press the sprayed, sticky side of the tape to the right side of the outer edges of one of the appliqué shapes. Let the tape extend ⅛ inch past the edges. The ends of each length of tape can overlap. To reduce bulk, start applying the tape at the center of a side rather than at a corner.

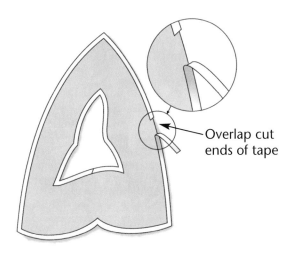

Overlap cut ends of tape

3. Set your machine for a zigzag stitch that's 2-mm long and wide. Using regular sewing thread, sew the inside edge of the tape to the appliqué. Clip along the curves. Use a pointcutter to trim off the corners, as shown in the illustration on page 24.

Finishing

A fast three-step process fuses, then stitches, the appliqué shapes to the garment.

1. Pin the appliqué shapes, right side up, to the right side of the garment. Move them around, overlapping and interlocking as desired. When all of the shapes are in position, continue to the next step.

2. If shapes overlap, remove the pins to release the bottom layer. Working only on the bottom shape, fold the taped edges to the wrong side. The fusible side of the tape is now against the garment. Fuse the edges to the garment, applying only enough pressure to glue them. Continue applying shapes on the lower layer, and then do the same with the subsequent

layers. When all of the shapes are fused to the garment, you're ready for the next step.

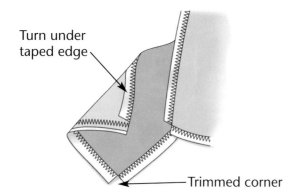

Turn under taped edge

Trimmed corner

3. Load invisible or matching thread in the needle and switch to a narrow zigzag stitch. (Use transparent thread if the color of the appliqué shapes varies.) Start with a 2-mm length and 1½-mm width. Place the work on the machine to start topstitching the appliqué shape to the garment along one edge. Turn the fly wheel by hand to ensure that the needle's left swing just catches the edge of the appliqué and the right swing is barely off the appliqué and in the garment fabric. If necessary, adjust the stitch width. Set the length so that it easily rounds curves and remains discreet. Use a longer stitch for dense or thick fabric. Sew around one fabric shape and then move on to the next.

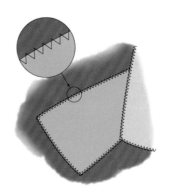

FAQ FREQUENTLY ASKED QUESTION

Won't fusing flatten the edges of appliqué shapes made from fabric that has nap or loft?

Use a lot of steam and ease up on the iron pressure. Instead, apply pressure with either your fingers or a wooden iron.

Lyla's Notion   Olfa Rotary Point Cutter

The first time that I saw this point cutter it was used to rip-out a seam. I purchased one, although I feared using it, because it was such a neat looking tool. It sat idle in my studio since I feared accidentally cutting through fabric along a seamline when using it.

Then came a situation I dreaded: clipping into a tight corner. There was a very distinct possibility that I'd damage the garment that I was making. My eyesight isn't what it used to be, so I often clipped through stitches when I snipped seam allowances with scissors. But I realized that the Olfa Rotary Point Cutter could reach into the seam allowance with great accuracy. Success was at hand.

To use the cutter, place the mat on a flat surface with the work on top. Position the point of the blade close to the stitching, at the beginning of the desired cutting line. Push down and roll the blade backward.

A miniature rotary cutter is the perfect solution for clipping corners and stitches. Precision is improved because a stationary blade with a point replaces the traditional free-wheeling circle.

Yet again function meets fashion. Finish the outer edges of one or both facings with a simple technique that transforms a garment necessity into a decorative element. Showcasing a facing on the outside of a garment and giving the edge an interesting shape is a fast way to add instant appeal to an otherwise plain garment.

Shaped Facing

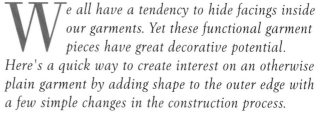

Asymmetrical Tunic & Skirt

W e all have a tendency to hide facings inside our garments. Yet these functional garment pieces have great decorative potential. Here's a quick way to create interest on an otherwise plain garment by adding shape to the outer edge with a few simple changes in the construction process.

You don't even need a garment with a facing pattern to create this effect. In fact, a lack of time and a tunic pattern that didn't have a front opening was the inspiration for this technique.

I had to leave for a consumer show in an hour, and absolutely had to make a jacket. My long-sleeve Asymmetrical Tunic pattern seemed suitable because it has only two pattern pieces. Rather than sewing up the front seam, I left it open and quickly drafted a facing pattern for one side. The opening edge on the other garment piece was simply turned under and topstitched.

Instead of hiding the facing on the inside, as most of us usually do, I brought it to the outside of the garment and added interesting shape along the edge. A single button holds the jacket together at the neck.

The technique for shaping and securing the outer edge came to me when I developed a neck finishing technique. (See page 89.) I can't believe the number of times that a single process I've developed has leapfrogged into an entirely new technique.

Supplies

Olfa Rotary Point Cutter

Sulky KK 2000 Temporary Adhesive Spray

Super Fine Fusible Bias Stay Tape

Wonder Invisible Thread (or matching embroidery)

Wooden iron* (optional)

*A 5- to 6-inch long piece of hardwood with a tapered end, used by quilters to press open ¼-inch wide seam allowances.

Suitable Fabric

This technique can be created on any fabric. However, plush fabric hides the edge stitching and contributes to the curved effect along the edges. The stitching is visible on smoother fabrics.

Shaping the Edge

Curves emerge as you apply bias tape along the outer edge of the facing.

1. Using your pattern piece, cut two facings from the fabric. Attach one to the garment front following the instructions for this technique, and then attach the remaining facing to the opposite front.

2. Apply adhesive spray to the non-fusible side of the Super Fine Fusible Bias Tape.

3. Finger-press the sprayed, sticky side of the bias tape to the right side of the outer edge of the facing. Shape the tape into gentle curves to establish the finished shape of the facing's outer edge.

4. Set your machine for a zigzag stitch that's 2-mm long and wide. Sew the inside edge of the tape to the facing. Trim the excess fabric from the edge of the facing, cutting along the edge of the bias tape. If necessary, clip through the seam allowances along the curves so the edges lay flat when turned.

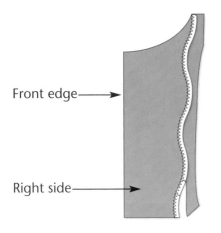

Front edge

Right side

Attaching the Facing

After the facing is sewn to the garment, the outer edge is turned under and fused to the front. All that's left to do is a bit of stitching to hold the pieces together at the outer edge.

1. Straight stitch the unshaped edge of the facing (side without bias tape) to the garment front with the right side of the facing to the wrong side of the garment.

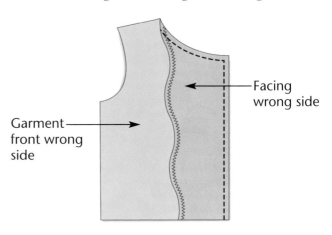

Garment front wrong side

Facing wrong side

2. Trim, grade, and clip the seam allowances.

3. Fold the facing to the right side of the garment front along the seamline.

4. Fold the taped edge to the wrong side of the facing. The fusible side of the bias tape is now against the garment front. Fuse the edge of the facing in place. For plush fabrics, use steam and fingertip pressure, or press the edge with a wooden iron.

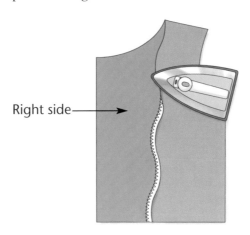

Right side

5. Load invisible thread in the needle and switch to a narrow zigzag stitch. Start with a 2-mm length and 2-mm width. Place the work on the machine to start topstitching the facing to the garment along the curved edge. Turn the fly wheel by hand to ensure that the needle's left swing just catches the edge of the facing and the right swing is barely off the facing and into the garment front. If necessary, adjust the stitch width.

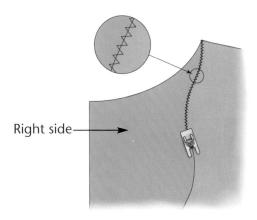

Right side

FREQUENTLY ASKED QUESTION

Is a zigzag stitch the only option for attaching the facing?

Absolutely not! Rather than trying to hide the stitching along the outer edge of the facing, you can play it up with decorative work, or simply edge stitch it in place.

inspiration point

try shaping the facing to echo the curves of a beautiful embroidered motif. I chalked the facing shape on the fabric and cut it out with enough excess material around the outline for hooping the fabric. (Because this particular piece is Polar Fleece and I didn't want to crush the fabric, I hooped water-soluble paper and then basted the fabric to the paper before stitching the motif. I also layered water–soluble paper on top, so that the stitching laid on the surface rather than sinking into the fabric.) After completing the embroidery, I cut the outer edge of the facing to match the shape of the embroidery motif.

Convertible Jacket

The yarns, ribbons, threads, and trims that dance across this vest fabric aren't embellishments in the traditional sense. The bits and pieces are actually the fabric because they're stitched to a grid of fabric strips. It's a bit of whimsy that works as an entire garment or just an accent. The work is so random that there's little chance of failure.

Rhapsody Fabric

Zea Vest Collection

How many spools of decorative thread do you have that aren't quite big enough for another project, yet are too precious to throw away? Now you can use them: Swirl the items on a fabric grid and secure the work with stitching. The finished product is material that you can make into a vest, scarf, or garment inset.

Rhapsody Fabric began as a friendly challenge. At a sewing exhibition, a woman asked me what she could create with a piece of cotton fabric full of evenly spaced square holes. It looked like a wooden trellis that gardeners use to support roses and other pretty plants. The "lattice cloth" was a remnant from a watercolor quilt kit that needed 2-inch fabric squares.

Back in my studio, I coupled the lattice cloth with water-soluble paper to create Rhapsody Fabric. Since few of us have access to lattice cloth, these instructions explain how to make your own grid from fabric strips or lengths of ribbon. It isn't until you look at the nubby finished fabric very closely that you see all of the leftovers.

Since Rhapsody Fabric is so easy to complete, it's a suitable project for all ages and all skill levels. I love teaching the technique in workshops because you can see the fabric and the creator. Personalities always come out in their fabric.

Supplies

¼-inch wide fabric strips, soft ribbon, or yarn

Bias edging (self fabric or contrast)

Decorative threads, lace, ribbon, ribbon floss, yarn, trim, and other ingredients for the "fabric"

Design Plus Water Soluble Paper (two pieces for each pattern shape)

Felt-tip fabric marker

Pencil

Rayon or metallic embroidery thread

Regular thread

Temporary adhesive spray

Selecting a Pattern

Rhapsody Fabric is suitable for entire garment pieces as well as overlays. Garments with simple lines and a minimum number of pattern pieces and seams are the best choice.

Decide which garment pieces will be made of Rhapsody Fabric. Avoid sleeves because the open material snags on jewelry and other items. Rhapsody Fabric looks great as the front of the Zea Vest or Sassy Jacket. Also consider Rhapsody Fabric for flaps, like the one on the long Zea Duster Vest, insets, overlays, and yokes. Patterns with bound edges are ideal. You don't have to worry about lining or hemming the edges of the Rhapsody Fabric, because the loose ends of the fabric ingredients are trapped inside the binding.

You can use a garment pattern that doesn't have bound edges, but a bit more work is involved. To prepare the garment pieces and ensure good fit, cut away all of the seam allowances along outer edges that you plan to bind.

Sassy Jacket adaptation

Making your own fabric is quick, fun, and a great way to use all the leftovers in your stash! The framework of the Rhapsody Fabric for this vest is built with cotton organdy ribbon. Many other fabrics, ribbons, and yarns are suitable for the grid.

Suitable Ingredients

Layering the ingredients on the background grid creates the fabric. The characteristics of each ingredient affect the drape and feel of the finished fabric.

Metallic threads make stiffer fabric. They're best used in combination with softer ingredients. Soft ribbon yields drapable fabric, but you can make it firmer by adding some stiffer items. Regular sewing thread works, but only if added to other, more substantial, ingredients.

The most interesting fabrics have ingredients in a range of sizes and weights. Consider the finished garment fabric requirements, and use ingredients that achieve the appropriate weight and thickness. A vest, for example, needs some body, but you don't want it stiff as a board. Consequently, you wouldn't use only metallic threads for the Rhapsody Fabric.

Preparing the Supplies

Most thread and yarns have minimal shrinkage, but you may need to pretreat some silk ribbons or other trims.

1. Working in batches, wind the ribbon and trims around your hand. (This prevents tangles.) Slide the wrapped ingredients off your hand and into a cup of hot water. Let the items sit, without agitating, until the water cools. Remove the items and let them air dry. Don't squeeze or scrunch the ingredients because they'll have wrinkles when dry.

2. Use a pencil to trace the pattern piece outline on a sheet of Design Plus Water Soluble Paper. If you're making a vest front, or other garment piece that needs matching shapes for the left and right side of the body, flip over the pattern piece and trace it a second time.

3. Cut out the shape 1 inch beyond the pattern outline.

Building the Fabric

Starting with a framework, apply layers of fabric ingredients. Symmetry is important when there are matching pattern pieces for the right and left side of the body: vest fronts, for example. Place the ingredients on both left and right pattern pieces at the same time.

1. Preshrink the ribbon, trim, yarn, or a firmly woven cotton fabric for the gridded framework. Cut the fabric into ¼-inch wide strips along the straight or crossgrain. Don't treat the raw fabric edges to prevent fraying because the stitching in later steps prevents much of this problem. Raveling isn't visible on the right side of the fabric.

2. Spray the top of the pattern-shaped water-soluble paper with a temporary adhesive like Sulky's KK 2000.

3. Press the framework on the sticky side of the water-soluble paper. Prevent a boxy appearance by scrunching the lengths of ribbon or fabric into irregular shapes. This makes the grid less visible in the finished piece.

4. Separate the fabric ingredients into heavy-, medium-, and lightweight categories.

5. The bulkiest ingredients are applied first. As they're covered by lighter weight items they'll command less attention. Part of the fabric's intrigue is the mystery of the ingredients. Swirl the bulkier ingredients evenly across the top of the framework. Make sure that all loose ends go into seam allowances. Apply progressively lighter weight items in each subsequent layer you add.

FREQUENTLY ASKED QUESTION

How many layers are enough?

This depends on the structure of the garment you're making. Do you need a soft, drapey Rhapsody Fabric (less ingredients), or a solid structured Rhapsody Fabric (more ingredients)? Let this be your guide. A lace fabric needs fewer layers than a heavier, stiffer piece of fabric.

6. As you build the layers, stop periodically to assess the overall appearance. Squint at the fabric. Wherever you see the water-soluble paper peeking through, there will be holes in your fabric. Continue adding layers until you like the look.

Securing the Layers

This is a great late-night process because you can stitch mindlessly without worrying about doing anything wrong!

1. Place another piece of water-soluble paper on top of the Rhapsody Fabric. Insert 5 or 6 pins through the paper and fabric to hold the "sandwich" in place while you carefully move all of the work off the table and over to the sewing machine.

2. If you like doing free–motion work, lower the feed dogs. Otherwise, keep the feed dogs engaged for this step. Set the machine for a straight, 3-mm long stitch and load the needle and bobbin with regular sewing thread. This is a great way to use all the short lengths of thread on bobbins and spools. Sew the layers together with a large swirling motion. Whenever you run out of thread, just rethread and continue stitching. Don't backstitch.

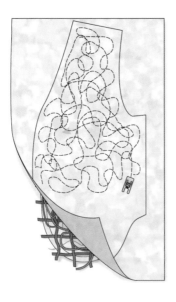

3. Continue stitching in a random swirling pattern. It isn't necessary to backstitch at the start and end of a stitching line. If you have an opening between two lines, try to cut it in half with the next line of stitching. This is a fun way to obtain evenly distributed stitching.

4. Stop sewing when the stitching lines are about ¾ inch apart.

Making the Garment Piece

The bulk of the fabric ingredients, and any small tucks made as you stitched, can distort the shape of the pattern piece. Now you need to fix this.

1. Anywhere you can see light through the paper there will be a hole in the finished fabric. Look for large holes and spaces that aren't as uniform as the rest of the fabric.

2. If you find a problem, place a few additional pieces of lightweight ingredients on top of the upper layer of water-soluble paper. Pull only the ends of the new ingredients to the wrong side of the Rhapsody Fabric. Spray adhesive on one side of a water-soluble paper patch. Place it on top of the new ingredients, and randomly stitch through all of the layers.

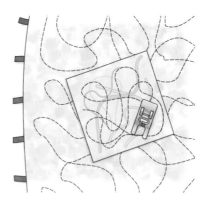

3. Use the felt-tip fabric marker to trace the pattern piece outline on the top layer of the Rhapsody Fabric. Also trace darts and other pattern markings.

inspiration point

Short fringe is easy to create on a piece of Rhapsody Fabric. Before removing the water-soluble stabilizer, decoratively stitch ½ inch away from—and parallel to—the edge where you want the fringe. After the water-soluble paper is removed from the garment, finger-comb the fringe to straighten the lengths. Use a rotary cutter and ruler to even the edges by cutting straight across the bottom.

Twister Scarf

---

4. Straight stitch along the outline that you just drew. This secures all the loose ends at the edges of the shape. Cut away the excess fabric just outside the stitching lines.

Assembling the Garment

Here's the ultimate motivation for completing a project: You can't reveal the Rhapsody Fabric until the garment is assembled.

Darts are sewn in the usual manner. Upon completion, fold the dart to one side, and stitch it down with a few straight stitches made in a swirl pattern. This flattens the dart and presses it into the background of the Rhapsody Fabric.

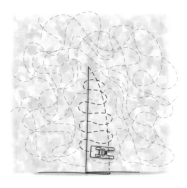

Seam allowances are sandwiched between garment fabric and a lining fabric for best results. To assemble a vest with a Rhapsody Fabric front, for example, sew the shoulder seam with the front sandwiched between the fabric garment back and back lining, with the raw edges even. When you flip the back and back lining away from the Rhapsody Fabric front, the seam allowances are trapped inside.

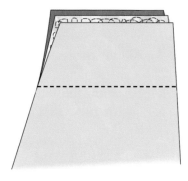

Bias Binding is a simple, efficient method to finish all edges that aren't part of a seam. Apply double fold binding with either fusible thread (the Lyla's Notion on page 41) or Ultra Soft Double Sided Fusible (the Lyla's Notion on page 76).

Revealing the Fabric

It's time to reveal your creation by removing the Design Plus Water Soluble Paper!

1. Submerge the garment in water. Use cold water if the fabric contains dark colors or silks and fine care ingredients. Warm water dissolves the water-soluble paper faster. Swish the material around to speed up the removal process. Add fresh water if it becomes too full of paper pulp.

2. The ingredients you used for the Rhapsody Fabric determine the most appropriate wash and care treatments for the garment. You can wash Rhapsody Fabric in a machine. Place the garment in a lingerie bag to prevent the fabric from catching on the agitator or closures on the garment. Use a gentle cycle.

inspiration point

rhapsody Fabric is the perfect background for embroidered motifs and decorative stitching. With the water-soluble paper still in place, simply pick an attractive location and start stitching.

Contrasting thread and a denser stitch are more visible on the Rhapsody Fabric. The water-soluble paper prevents the decorative stitching from sinking into the background layers.

The embroidery on the Rhapsody Fabric overlay, at right, was stitched with a light color thread.

The name of this technique is one of my favorites. Rhapsody is derived from rhaptein, which means to sew or stitch together a miscellaneous collection.

Zea Vest Collection

Listen to your fabric. If you take advantage of its characteristics you can create the most exciting work. The simplicity of Sculpted Appliqué is a perfect example of a technique that takes advantage of the characteristics of a material. In this case, it's felted and plush non-woven fabrics.

Sculpted Appliqué

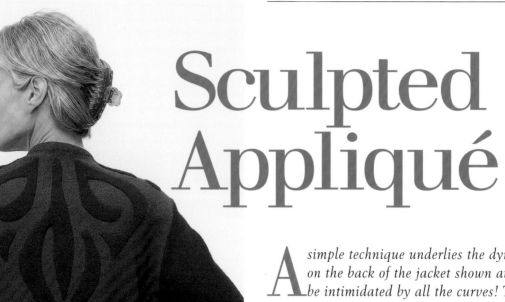

Sassy Jacket

A simple technique underlies the dynamic shapes on the back of the jacket shown at left. Don't be intimidated by all the curves! They're not as challenging as you might assume because they're made with a no-muss, no-fuss technique. Simply cut a single-layer design from non-woven fabric and stitch it to a background fabric. Since the edges of the appliqué shapes used for the design don't ravel, there's no need to turn under the seam allowances.

This technique is the result of a happy accident. I originally planned an invisible appliqué with two beautiful pieces of hand-felted knit wool. But my test samples didn't turn out as anticipated. I found that rather than looking like an appliqué, the effect was sculptural. When complete, the stitching buried the edges of the appliqué in the background fabric, so it looked like the shape was built up from the base.

Without close inspection, students in my classes don't realize that the Sculpted Appliqué samples that I display involve applying one layer of non-woven plush fabric to another. The technique is similar to Faux Trapunto on page 113, but simpler and less time-consuming. To create a Sculpted Appliqué, one layer is placed on a single layer fabric background. If working with smoother fabrics, use the Faux Trapunto technique for the best results. (Mind you, the trapunto shapes are limited to motifs that can be created with bias fabric tubes.)

Supplies

Open toe presser foot (optional)

Pattern tracing paper

Sulky KK 2000 Temporary Adhesive Spray

YLI Wonder Transparent Thread (clear or smoke)

Convertible Jacket

Polar Fleece, boiled wool, and other similar fabrics are good choices because they don't ravel, and have body and volume. Both the appliqué and the garment need to be made from a plush (squishy) fabric.

Creating a Design

Shapes that you can use for an appliqué are all around us. The motif on page 34 comes from a business card. I enlarged and rounded one side of the design and slightly adjusted the shape to fit on my garment pattern pieces.

You can make a sculpted appliqué with any shape: all-over design or as an accent for a garment. If your appliqué is several pieces of fabric, they can overlap.

It's easiest to apply the appliqué to a flat fabric background. This doesn't mean you have to attach it to a single garment piece. The work looks attractive going over a seam, like the center back or a shoulder, for example.

Decide where you want to place the appliqué on the garment. If necessary, assemble the garment pieces until you have completed the seam that will be covered. If the appliqué goes on a single garment piece, no garment construction is required before attaching the sculpture.

Lyla's Notion   Sulky KK 2000

Temporary adhesive is great because it eliminates the use of pins and basting. It instantly transforms an appliqué, trim, or bias into a stick-on version by evenly applying the spray and it can also be used to hold together fabric layers.

KK 2000 is my favorite brand. I think it's great because it doesn't gum up the needle, and it gets extra points for being ozone-friendly. Its strength is about the same as a Post-It note. The effect wears off, so plan to complete your project within a few days.

As you read other sections of this book, you'll see that I use the adhesive spray for many of the techniques. It's helpful during the construction of Rhapsody Fabric and makes it a breeze to apply shapes for the Instant Appliqué process. Curved Piecing and Shaped Facings would be much more difficult without the help of a temporary adhesive spray.

Apply this adhesive spray to a fabric appliqué or trim that needs to be temporarily secured to a fabric background. The layer stays in place without pins, and can be repositioned.

Preparing the Appliqué

This pin-less process is a breeze. Merely cut out the appliqué and spray it with adhesive.

1. Trace your desired design on pattern tracing paper. Trim the paper along the design lines to make your pattern.

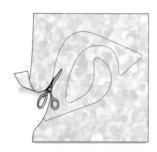

2. Cut the exact appliqué shape from the fabric. Don't add seam allowances.

3. Apply Sulky KK 2000 Temporary Adhesive Spray to the wrong side of the appliqué.

Convertible Jacket

The plush side of the fabric is used again, this time as a shaped facing. (See page 25.) When planning a garment, don't hesitate to apply more than one technique to achieve continuity from the front to the back.

Positioning the Appliqué

It's a good idea to step back from your design and look at the work the way that people around you will see the finished piece. An overview identifies problems before the appliqué is permanently attached to the background.

1. Press the appliqué onto the fabric background at the planned position.

Raw fabric edge

2. Put the partially finished garment on a hanger and hang it on a wall. Step back, preferably more than four feet, and examine the piece. (It can look very different from a distance or another perspective.)

3. Move the appliqué around on the garment until you're happy with the appearance.

Attaching the Appliqué

The sculpted look evolves as you invisibly stitch the raw edges of the appliqué to the background fabric.

1. Thread your machine with transparent thread, unless you have a regular thread that matches the appliqué color perfectly. Adjust the stitch to a 2-mm long and 2-mm wide zigzag. Make the stitch as narrow as possible, so that the left and right swing of the needle just catch the appliqué and garment fabrics. Don't make the stitch so narrow that the needle misses the appliqué edges.

2. Zigzag the appliqué to the garment. If the stitching is slightly visible when complete, run your fingernail along the edge to make the fabric fluff around the stitching.

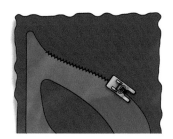

Is there an easy way to stitch around corners and curves?

Stop with the needle down when it swings to the right. Pivot the work and continue stitching. This prevents an uneven gap between the stitches at the outside edge of the appliqué.

Lyla's Notion — YLI Wonder Invisible Thread

This versatile product works well with a wide variety of fabrics. It's ideal when you want thread to disappear into a multi-color or pieced fabric. There's no dilemma deciding which color to match, and you don't need to change thread as you sew across each color or section on the fabric. There are two versions of transparent thread; use smoke for dark fabrics and clear for light-color material.

The elasticity of transparent thread, used in the needle, is specially helpful with some techniques, particularly when you're doing decorative bobbin stitching with a heavy thread that you want to sit nicely on the fabric.

By using transparent thread in the needle, you don't have to adjust the tension dial. The needle thread automatically pulls the heavier bobbin thread to the fabric surface. This happens because, as it travels through the upper tension, the thread pulls taut. However, if you need a balanced stitch when working with transparent thread, slightly loosen the upper tension.

Invisible thread is a sewing supply essential. It's the perfect solution when a beautiful fabric needs invisible stitching for an embellishment and when a good matching thread can't be found.

A variety of looks can be achieved, depending on your stitch and thread selection, as well as your fabric choice. This is one place you'll want to give yourself time to play to find the perfect combination for your project.

YLI Wonder Invisible Thread washes well and can be dry-cleaned. Avoid ironing over the thread. It's nylon so it can melt. Use a press cloth.

A simplified method of random curved piecing creates an unusual look that allows you to combine various fabrics into one special piece. What a great way to use fabric scraps to create a coordinating material! On the dress at left, the front panel below the bodice visually lengthens the body, which is a nice way to add slimming lines to a garment.

Shanley

Curved Piecing

Like a quilter building new material from smaller pieces, you can develop an entirely new fabric. But unlike quilting, the Curved Piecing technique is simple and requires little planning. Even though the curved seamlines look complex, you don't have to cut out pattern pieces or fabric shapes, nor do you need to add seam allowances. Just start with one fabric scrap, attach it to another, and continue building the fabric until the work is large enough to accommodate your pattern piece. This is really a series of random, happy accidents.

Part of the assembly process includes edge stitching near the seamlines. On my Shanley dress, at left, I used a subtle decorative stitch by the seam. The accent adds variety without intruding on the overall appearance of the garment. On other garments I pull out all the stops: using several decorative stitches and threads for the pieced seams on a whimsical pocket, for example.

Yardage made from curved piecing has many applications. It can be used as a panel or edging, an overlay on a garment, or as an entire garment piece. For a first project, consider making something small, like a pocket and cuffs. I've used Curved Piecing for a tunic front, and also as a panel on a straight skirt. On a wrap skirt, a 5- or 6-inch wide strip of curved, pieced fabric looks great along the loose vertical edge.

Supplies

Decorative thread (optional)

Matching thread

Mini Iron (optional)

Olfa Rotary Point Cutter (optional)

Sulky KK 2000 Temporary Adhesive Spray

Super Fine Bias Stay Tape

Suitable Fabric Pieces

Many fabric weights are suitable, but keep them compatible for any given garment. Look for similar weights, drapes, and washing instructions. It's best to use shapes that are no smaller than 4 inches square.

Making a Seam

Pretend you're building a puzzle: connecting two pieces, and adding another—and even more scraps—until you're finished. The fabric shapes can vary, but make sure that joined edges are all the same length.

1. Choose two fabric rectangles or squares. Select an edge on each. The two selected edges are the ones that you join in subsequent steps. Cut these edges to the same length. (If preferred, you can trim the edges after they're stitched together in a later step.)

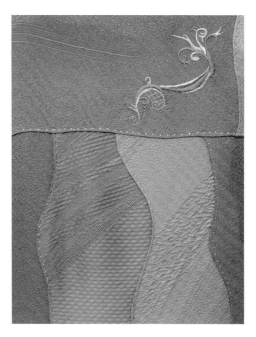

This is the back of the dress shown on page 38. Continuity is established by using the same fabrics, decorative edge stitch, and thread. However, the size, shape, and placement of the fabric pieces are different. An embroidered motif adds a nice finishing touch.

Lyla's Notion   Super Fine Bias Stay Tape

Super Fine Bias Stay Tape is extremely lightweight and virtually undetectable in seams. Since it doesn't add bulk while it stabilizes, it's an ideal product for many applications. The lengths are cut on the half-bias, so it's a stable product that still has enough give to smoothly travel around shapes and curves.

In Curved Piecing, the Super Fine Bias Tape helps create a flight of fancy. Mind you, I also like to use the product for functional sewing, like stabilizing curved neck edges.

I like the ⅜-inch wide Super Fine Bias Tape because it's wide enough to handle easily. Since one side is fusible, you don't need stitching to secure it to fabric. Just place it in position, and then fuse it down with an iron.

The many characteristics of this 100% polyester tape are ideal for a stress-free Curved Piecing session at your sewing machine.

The flexibility of bias and the lightweight nature of this stay tape is ideal for applications wherever extra bulk would detract from a garment's drape. Super Fine Bias Stay Tape isn't cut on a perfect bias, so it has a bit of stability.

2. Cut a length of Super Fine Bias Tape a few inches longer than one of the "joining" edges. Spray adhesive on the non-fusible side of the tape. Hold the can directly above the tape as you spray the appropriate side of the length of the tape. Working in this manner prevents the force of the spray from flipping the tape as you apply the adhesive to it.

3. Finger-press the sprayed side of the tape to the right side of the first fabric piece, along the edge that will be joined. Gently curve the tape as you press it to the fabric. Let the tape extend ⅛ inch past the beginning and end of the edge.

4. Set your machine for a 2-mm wide and long zigzag stitch. Sew the inside edge of the tape to the piece of fabric. Trim the excess fabric along the edge of the tape and clip curves where necessary. I avoid cutting too far by using an Olfa Rotary Point Cutter. This point cutter is a handy tool to have in your sewing kit. It functions much like a rotary cutter. I frequently use mine when precise cutting is necessary. To learn more about the gadget, see the photo and complete description in the Lyla's Notion feature on page 24.

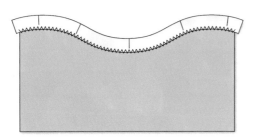

5. With right sides up, place the curved edge at the bottom of a second piece of fabric. Turn under the tape along the curved edge so that the fusible side is face down on the second fabric. Fuse the tape with the tip of an iron or Mini Iron. Apply only enough pressure to "glue" the fabric edges. Overlap the upper, curved, edge on the second fabric by at least ⅜ inch. Without fabric underneath the tape, it sticks to the ironing board.

6. Secure the joined edges with a line of stitching next to the curved edge, through all fabric layers. You can use a decorative or straight stitch and decorative or matching thread. Trim excess fabric behind the seam.

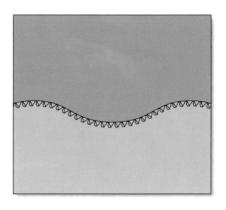

FAQ   FREQUENTLY ASKED QUESTION

Changing thread and stitch selection for every seam is a hassle. Is there a shortcut?

Stitch and fuse an entire row of pieces together (Steps 1 to 5 on page 39 and this page). Now switch to a decorative thread and edge stitch along the seams. If you're lucky enough to own two machines, you can set each machine differently and move from one to the other.

Adding More Pieces

Continue adding fabric pieces, following the steps in "Making a Seam" (page 39) until the pieced work is long enough to accommodate the pattern piece.

With each new seam, I like to add visual interest by alternating the direction of the start of the curve. Start by joining several pieces of fabric, and then add another to the opposite edge. This ensures that one end of the previous line of stitching ends up in a seam allowance. You won't have to backstitch at the start and end of each stitching line.

Make sure that the pieced sections aren't all similar widths, so it looks like you tried to make them identical but didn't succeed. Instead, try making a row of several small joined fabric shapes, and then attach the group to a larger fabric piece.

To create a wider piece, simply add fabric pieces to one or both sides of the existing work.

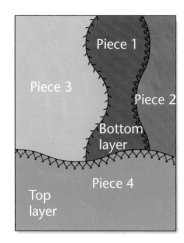

Lyla's Notion   Fusible Thread

Like regular sewing thread, fusible thread can be used in your sewing machine. The thread works best in the bobbin because its texture is too rough for the needle. Wind the thread on to the bobbin by machine, just like you would regular thread. Set the machine for a long stitch length. This is important, because only thread that is sitting on top of the fabric will act as a bonding agent.

After stitching, apply heat, steam, and pressure to the stitching line to melt the fusible thread so that it fuses the layers.

Quite a bit of pressure is required to fuse the thread, so it is best used on fabrics without a lot of volume. Bulky fabrics like Polar Fleece or wool tend to flatten during pressing, so they are not a good choice. Also avoid fabrics that have a rough, loosely woven surface.

I often use fusible thread when binding a garment. Pin together the right sides of the binding strip and the garment. With fusible thread in the bobbin and the binding facing up, stitch ⅜ inch from the edge.

Fusible thread is a fast and easy way to baste fabric pieces. I love using it to fuse trim and binding to garment pieces before permanently stitching them in position. You can ensure that a binding is an even-width along an entire edge and prevent layers of fabric or trim from shifting during sewing.

Logically, the next step is wrapping the binding around the fabric edge and pinning it in place. Fusible thread eliminates this step. Instead, at the ironing board, roll the binding strip to the wrong side of garment while turning under the raw edge. The folded edge should just cover the row of fusible thread that is visible on the wrong side of the garment. As you turn the binding to the wrong side, fuse a small section in place with the tip of the iron. Continue fusing until all of the binding is fused in place.

From right side of garment, secure the binding with edge stitching (or stitch-in-the-ditch) close to the seamline.

Galleria Jacket

Kinsey Jacket

Dimension & Details

Sassy Jacket

Inspiration is everywhere. This is part of the reason working with fabric and design is so captivating. I don't have to be in my studio for something to trigger an idea. Garment shopping in boutiques is one of my favorite sources because one good store is enough to fill a notebook.

Imagine puckered pant legs leading to a terrific textured fabric called Hills & Valleys (page 47), or a 5-cent garage sale find adding interest to hand-painted, watercolor silk (Grate Detailing on page 55).

These techniques, like all of the ones featured in the next 26 pages, start with a flat, basic fabric and end with a unique piece of yardage that has dimension and texture. There are all-over techniques suitable for an entire garment, while other fabrics look best as accent pieces. All open the door to a fresh, boutique look. Add, reconfigure, accent, assemble, or decorate the surface for a personalized effect.

Elastic texturizing is a great way to add visual interest to a garment, or even draw in the back waist. Randomly placed gathers make the fabric in this Outback Jacket as enticing as it feels. There was a time when I wondered why on earth I purchased the yardage. The answer was at my fingertips, because it's a soft, luxurious microfiber.

Elastic Texturizing

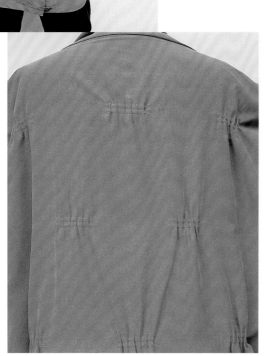

Outback Jacket

T his technique could be called *Sleepless in Nevada*, since that's how I came up with the idea to add all-over interest to fabric by applying small lengths of a special tape called *Stitch'n Stretch Elastic*.

A few days before my discovery, I saw a similar effect on a coat. I played around with elastic and fabric, to see if I could come up with a technique. Although I achieved an attractive effect, a simple process eluded me.

Perhaps it's true that inspiration sneaks up on you when you least expect it, for the answer came to me when I should have been counting sheep. *Stitch'n Stretch Elastic* allowed me to quickly and easily draw in the fabric. At first I applied the idea to gathering the back waist of a vest for a pattern that I was developing.

From this strictly functional use, I graduated to a purely decorative, all-over texture design. This is what I'm going to teach you to create, although you can use the same instructions for elasticizing the back of a vest or dress.

Supplies

Chalk, pencil, or air/water-erasable fabric marking pen

Stitch'n Stretch Elastic, width as desired

Suitable Fabric

Fabric with a soft hand works best. I've had success with rayon, silk, tencel, microfiber, and soft cotton. Use a lightweight interfacing. This won't interfere with the tape texturizing unless it makes the fabric hard or crisp.

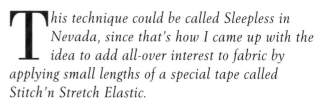

Choosing a Pattern

When considering a garment for this technique, think about how much ease is in the pattern. The jacket shown on page 44 is loose fitting. I wasn't concerned about losing ½ inch here or there on the garment by adding the elastic since the jacket is loose enough to still fit well. I cut the garment shapes from the fabric, and then did my texturizing. When I choose a more closely fitted pattern I slightly adjust the process, as explained in the following steps, so that the finished garment fits.

1. Trace the pattern piece on the fabric. Remove the pattern piece from the fabric. Cut out the shape, leaving several inches of fabric extending beyond all of the edges of the pattern piece.

2. Apply the texturizing effect to the fabric pattern piece.

3. Once you're happy with the texturizing, you're ready to adjust the garment shape. Lay the tissue pattern piece on the fabric and cut out the exact pattern shape.

Planning Elastic Placement

Let the fabric, the shape of the finished garment, and your creativity guide the placement of the texturizing. Gathering is controlled entirely by the length and position of the elastic pieces.

Elastic texturizing draws attention, so don't place it on any part of the garment that corresponds with a trouble spot on your body. Likewise, avoid the bust point. Don't position texturizing close to seam and garment edges as it can distort the garment shape.

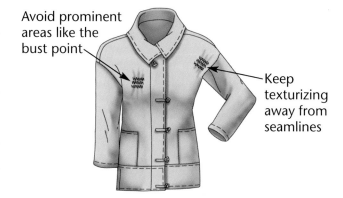

Avoid prominent areas like the bust point

Keep texturizing away from seamlines

Lyla's Notion — Stitch'n Stretch Elastic

Stitch'n Stretch elastic was primarily used as a waistband treatment when it was introduced. That's how I first applied it to a garment, but I no longer recommend this use. The elastic adds visual bulk, which isn't very flattering. Besides, the elastic doesn't wear well in high stress areas like a waistband.

For other functional and decorative uses, I really like this product. It's great for shaping vest backs (see page 46), creating an overall texture on fabric, or making faux ribbed waistbands and cuffs (see page 6).

The elastic is sewn flat to the wrong side of the fabric, eliminating the need to stretch and sew at the same time. It's extremely simple to work with. You draw in the elastic after it's applied to the fabric, which gives you the opportunity to fine tune the amount of gathering on your garment piece after it's stitched.

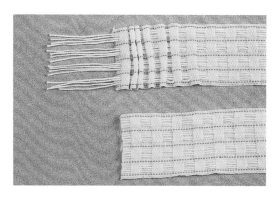

Stitch'n Stretch elastic is actually a tape with elastic cords woven through the length. Blue guides between the cords show you where to stitch.

For symmetrical texturizing, like the jacket back on page 44, place the elastic in the center of a garment piece and add more lengths by working toward the sides.

The elastic is horizontal on the jacket, although it would be just as easy to vary the positions. Consider making a chevron (upside-down V) from two pieces of elastic.

It's easiest to sew elastic to a garment piece before attaching the fabric shape to another. However, if you want texturizing across a seam, you need to sew and press it before attaching the elastic.

Applying the Elastic

This is the easiest part of the project. All you have to do is stitch the flat elastic to the wrong side of the fabric, draw it up, and secure the ends.

1. At one location for the texturizing, decide how long you want the gathered area to be when it's finished. Cut a piece of elastic 2 inches longer. Beauty is in the eye of the beholder, although a 2- to 5-inch finished length works well. The longer the length of elastic, however, the more fabric you have to pull up. Consider smaller lengths for more fitted garments. The jacket has 3-inch finished lengths.

2. On the wrong side of the fabric, draw a line to help you position the top of the elastic.

3. Pin the elastic to the wrong side of the garment piece, with the upper edge on the placement line. Center the elastic at the desired location.

4. Straight stitch the elastic to the garment piece by sewing along the blue guides in the elastic using a 3 to 3.5 mm stitch length. You don't have to use all of the lines. I stitched five lines on the vest shown on this page, but only three on the jacket shown on page 44. Don't stitch the first and last inch at the short ends of the elastic.

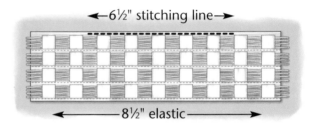

5. Cut off the excess cords. Fold under the raw edge of the elastic at one loose end. Fold it again, so that the end won't ravel. Stitching only through the tape, sew along the end through all thicknesses using a 1 to 1.5 mm length. This stitching does not show on the outside of the garment, so sew until you are sure that the elastic cords will stay in place.

6. Pull the cords at the opposite end of the elastic until the fabric is drawn in the desired amount. Secure the remaining end.

The elastic for the vest back shown above is 6-inches long, pulled in to 5 inches.

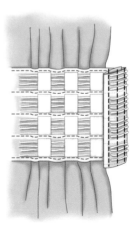

From ordinary to extraordinary, the Hills and Valleys technique converts normal fabric into a custom piece that's covered with decorative stitching and texture. This process also builds some give into the fabric. The effect is superb for entire garments, yokes, sleeves, bodices, jacket fronts, vests, fabric belts, and cuffs.

Hills and Valleys

Sassy Jacket

Not all inspiration comes from well-executed garments. In fact, an odd pair of pants led to the Hills and Valleys technique. Arriving early for a concert at Lake Tahoe, I had time to check out the fashions in some boutiques. (Needless to say, browsing among the clothing racks is one of my favorite pastimes).

As I was looking on one rack, I spotted a pair of pants across the aisle. They screamed "Cheap!" because the fabric was puckered.

Since the store was full of expensive clothing, I investigated. The puckering that I thought was poor construction turned out to be an attempt at creating interest on the fabric.

The idea was sound, even if the execution wasn't. I had my mission.

The concept for this technique is creating a single textured fabric from two plain pieces of yardage. The main fashion fabric (upper or surface layer) is pre-shrunk and then stitched to a backing fabric that isn't pre-shrunk. When washed and dried, only the backing fabric shrinks, thus pulling up the fashion fabric for a unique appearance that reminds me of hills and valleys.

Supplies

Embroidery thread

Pencil, chalk, or air/water-erasable fabric marking pen

Quilter's guide-bar

Quilter's ruler

Rotary cutter

Silk straight pins (optional, see "Laying Out the Fabric" Step 3, page 49)

Temporary spray adhesive (optional, see the FAQ on page 53)

Water-soluble thread

Suitable Fabric

Choosing appropriate fabrics is extremely important. Consider the colorfastness, drapability, hand, shrinkage, and wrinkle resistance of the fabrics. Working with test samples is the easiest way to evaluate your upper and base fabric selections.

Since this technique requires processing both fabrics in hot water, making test samples is critical. You may discover that a fabric you would never consider processing in hot water and a hot clothes dryer works well. Remember, you only have to wash this way a few times because the finished garment is treated as a fine washable.

The upper (fashion) fabric shows on the outside of the finished garment. A light- to medium-weight material is the best choice. The lighter the fabric weight, the more texture you achieve. Rayons, light- to medium-lightweight silks, and polyester silkies are all fabrics that work well.

Just because a fabric says, "dry clean only," that doesn't mean it can't be washed. Many fabrics can be washed in hot water even if you might not be inclined to wash that way on a regular basis. The key here is to experiment.

I devised a shrinkage test to help with this process. (See page 53.) If you plan to stitch with a contrasting thread, sew the thread on to the fabric before washing. This determines if the fabric dye bleeds on to the thread and changes its color.

The base fabric lies under the upper, fashion fabric so it doesn't show on the outside of the garment. It's responsible for causing the finished texture. My favorite choice is 100% cotton interlock. Don't hesitate to try single knits, or woven fabrics that you think will shrink. This is one of the only situations where I use bargain fabrics. Often, the less expensive interlocks are more loosely knit so they shrink more. This is not guaranteed. Wash a sample and make your own decision.

The more the base fabric shrinks, the better. If it's heavier than the upper yardage, the finished effect is more textured than the appearance of a piece made with similar-weight base and fashion fabrics.

A great time to test the base fabric is when you're experimenting with the upper fabric. Use the same technique and measurements. Make sure the color of the base fabric isn't visible through the upper fabric. Testing the base and upper fabrics together will also allow you to check for any color transfer.

Do not pre-shrink the base fabric before stitching. This texturizing effect relies on the natural shrinkage of the base fabric to achieve the dimensional look.

Yardage

The amount of fabric you need is affected by many variables: the amount of stitching, fabric type, and grainline position of the fabric layers. To be safe, figure on 25% more yardage than usual. For example, if your pattern calls for 1 yard, get 1¼ yards.

FAQ FREQUENTLY ASKED QUESTION

A yardage estimate is great, but is there a way to be more specific?

Instructions to test shrinkage, and yardage formulas based on the results, are on page 54. Make sure that you use hot water and a hot dryer, regardless of the care instructions for the fabric.

I urge you to do this test, even if you don't want to calculate yardage. Testing solves challenges before you launch a project. There's always a design innovation if you are a little short on fabric, or it doesn't turn out as anticipated. Spend less time worrying about what might happen, and more time in the doing. You'll enjoy your creative time more! Happy accidents can make your garment look even better.

Preparing the Upper Fabric

There are many variables with this technique. It's vital that you test your combination of fabrics and stitches.

1. Pre-wash the *upper fabric only* in hot water and detergent, and dry it in a hot dryer. Repeat the washing and drying process again. This step ensures that the upper fabric shrinks as much as possible before stitching. You don't want the upper fabric to shrink at all at a later step in this technique, when it's attached to the base fabric and washed again in hot water. During the last wash-and-dry only the lower fabric layer should shrink.

2. Mark the right side of the fashion fabric with vertical and horizontal lines to create stitching guides. (Later, you make a decorative stitch wherever the lines intersect.) For your first project, consider a 1-inch grid using chalk, a marking pencil or air/water-erasable fabric marking pen.

Rather than drawing a grid across the entire fabric surface, you can use a quilter's guide-bar. Simply mark one vertical and one horizontal line on your fabric. At the sewing machine, set your guide-bar 1 inch from the needle. Thread your needle and bobbin with water-soluble thread and baste the grid lines. Just make sure that the previous line of stitching is underneath the guide-bar extension when making the next line. The grid lines wash away when you wash the fabric piece to shrink it.

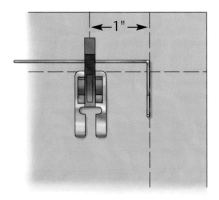

Laying Out the Fabric

The position of the fabric layers affects the pattern of the finished texture. If your base fabric is a knit, then the amount of built-in stretch that you achieve in the finished yardage is also affected.

1. Check the test swatch to see if the base fabric shrank more along the width or length. Shrinkage is usually greater along the length so the following steps are based on this result. If the fabric width shrank more, then reverse the suggested positions. (The direction that shrinks the most gives you the most stretch in the finished fabric.)

2. Decide if you want most of the give in your fabric to be vertical or horizontal on your pattern piece. To create vertical stretch, place the upper fabric on top of the base fabric with both grainlines parallel.

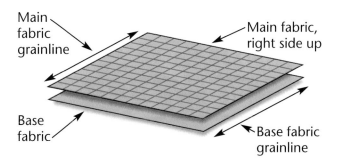

Main fabric grainline

Main fabric, right side up

Base fabric

Base fabric grainline

To create crosswise stretch in your finished fabric, place the upper fabric on top of the base fabric with the grainlines perpendicular.

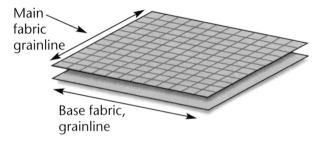

Main fabric grainline

Base fabric, grainline

3. Temporarily join the fabric layers. You can pin the base and upper fabric layers together every 6 to 8 inches. (I use long silk pins.) Another option is applying a temporary adhesive spray to the top of the base fabric and then adding the upper layer. You can also baste the two layers together with lines of water-soluble thread stitched every 10 to 12 inches.

Choosing a Stitch

Set aside the base and upper fabric layers. It's time to play with the stitches on your machine. The goal is to select a stitch or pattern that holds the fabric layers together and forces the upper fabric to texturize when the piece is washed.

The appearance of the finished piece depends on your equipment. While you can use a sewing machine that has only utility stitches, decorative work and long basting stitches make a world of difference.

You can stitch together the fabric layers along all of the grid lines or the fabric can be tacked together at the intersections of the grid lines. The wrinkling tends to be more pronounced with tacking, but I have seen exceptions. On an electronic machine, select a single pattern stitch. If you have a mechanical machine, you can make several short, straight stitches, or a bar tack, at each intersection.

The longer the stitch length, the more the fabric seems to shift, and the more texture you see. Here are some ideas for combining stitches on the grid.

Sassy Jacket

This jacket is from my collection of patterns. All of my designs are intended to be figure-flattering and versatile, but I also develop them with my techniques in mind. The lapel on the Sassy Jacket, for example, is the perfect location for Hills and Valleys texturizing.

A simple straight stitch along the grid lines, with a decorative stitch every 1 to 1¼ inches.

A programmed stitch yields wonderful results. You can use straight basting stitches along the grid lines with a decorative stitch every 1 to 1¼ inches. Pull out the basting after stitching all the lines.

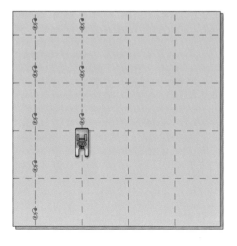

A utility stitch also makes interesting texture. Lengthen it until you like the appearance, and then stitch row after row or apply a grid pattern.

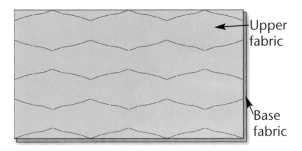

Upper fabric

Base fabric

A combination of pattern stitches connected by straight stitching.

Take advantage of your machine's ability to program stitches. Consider combining a straight stitch with a decorative stitch. You can sew each row in a continuous line. This eliminates marking a grid on the upper fabric if you have a quilter's guide-bar.

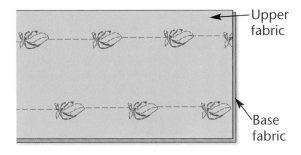

Upper fabric

Base fabric

Larger, all-over designs take the concept a step further. Draw the design (or use an embroidery design) on your fabric, and then stitch it randomly on the fabric surface. Avoid dense stitch patterns because they aren't as successful.

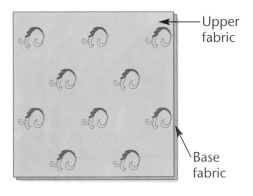

Upper fabric

Base fabric

FREQUENTLY ASKED QUESTION

What's the best way to create a successful stitch combination?

I can't emphasize "experiment" too often. Test your stitch selections on a swatch of layered fabrics. Process the finished sample in hot water with detergent, and then finish it in a dryer. Check the sample for drapability, as well as for wrinkling, colorfastness, and the texture pattern. You can make several small samples, process them together, and choose your favorite. Some stitch will create a dynamite piece of fabric!

Changing the stitch pattern changes the direction of the wrinkles on the finished fabric. The direction of the wrinkles can also be adjusted by changing the grainlines of the upper and base fabrics. In general, the wrinkle tends to form between the stitching, in the opposite direction of the grain of the base fabric.

Parallel grainlines for the base and upper fabrics give you a horizontal wrinkle pattern when there is stitching at every intersection of a 1-inch grid.

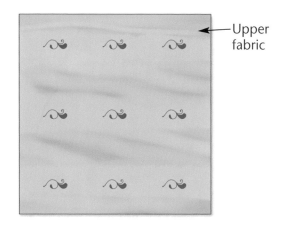

Upper fabric

On the other hand, if you stitch at each intersection when the fabrics are joined with the grainlines perpendicular, your wrinkle pattern will be vertical.

Perpendicular grainlines for the base and upper fabrics give you a vertical wrinkle pattern.

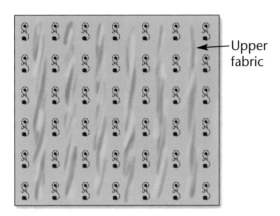

Upper fabric

Alternate stitch positions so that each intersection is stitched every other row. The wrinkles randomly jog up and down across the fabric. The results are similar, regardless of the position of the grainlines.

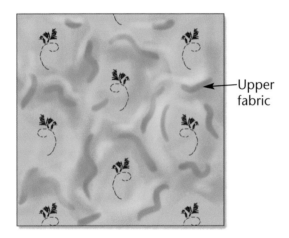

Upper fabric

Stitching the Fabric Layers

The fun part of this project is the experimenting that we've already done (although I do enjoy seeing the results on the finished yardage). Now we're close to completing the project. Layering the fabrics, adding the surface stitching, and treating the yardage takes no time at all.

1. Place the fashion fabric on top of the base fabric with the wrong sides together. Temporarily join them with rows of long, straight stitches and water-soluble thread. I usually make vertical and horizontal rows of basting, but it depends on the fabric. Slippery and other hard-to-handle fabrics are definitely stitched in both directions and I frequently use the spray adhesive before basting, for extra security.

If you already basted grid lines to the upper fabric with water-soluble thread, follow these same lines to join the fabric layers.

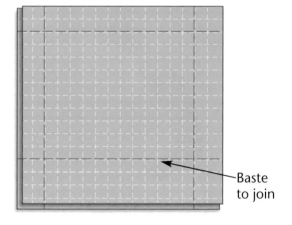

Baste to join

Hills and Valleys yardage is soft and drapable, although results can vary. Every finished fabric has unique characteristics that are determined by the fabric selected, the stitches and thread used, and the shrinking process.

FREQUENTLY ASKED QUESTION

Is there an easier way to hold the fabric layers together?

You can spray the wrong side of one fabric with a temporary adhesive. Some adhesives only last a few days so choose this option only if you are planning to complete your decorative stitching in that time frame. Pin–basting works just as well. Pin as infrequently as possible, say every 6 to 8 inches. Make sure the pinpoints are pushed through to the back of the fabric to prevent pinpricks as you work. There's no need to pin around the perimeter.

2. Following the marked grid, add your permanent decorative, utility, or straight stitches to the fabric layers as planned.

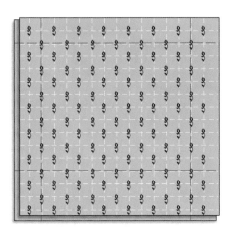

3. Shrink the joined fabrics by processing them in hot water, with detergent, and a hot clothes dryer. Repeat the process.

4. Cut the garment pattern pieces from your new Hills and Valleys yardage. Now all you have to do is assemble them as usual.

Fabric Shrinkage and Yardage Estimating

There are many times where it's beneficial to know how much a fabric shrinks before you process the entire yardage. You learn, for example, if the fabric wrinkles or changes hand.

If a fabric shrinks a lot, I can figure out if I have enough yardage for my project. And the way that a processed fabric drapes tells me if it will work for the garment that I have in mind. The test even helps me avoid dry cleaning costs. Many fabrics marked as "dry clean only" can be washed successfully, as long as the yardage is washed and dried before construction begins.

Kanisha

Any time you're worried that a new fabric will shrink too much, you can perform a simple test. Although the fabric in the outfit above doesn't have a texturizing treatment, the test was still beneficial because it helped determine whether there was enough fabric.

To keep the process simple, it's important to cut fabric to specific dimensions and then create a template of that piece before it's processed. Compare the processed piece to the template, and you immediately know the amount that the fabric shrinks. Hold the fabric and drape it over your hand to determine the drapability, check for wrinkling, and make other necessary inspections.

Making the Sample

1. Cut a piece of fabric that's 10 inches along the lengthwise grain and 5 inches wide along the crosswise grain. Serge the raw edges.

2. Place the fabric rectangle on a piece of 8½ x 11-inch paper and trace around the perimeter.

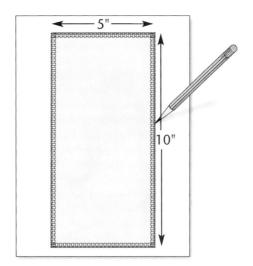

3. Wash and dry the fabric rectangle at least once. Use the same processing that applies to the finished garment, or according to the needs of a specific technique. Refer to the step-by-step technique instructions in this book for guidance. A test swatch for the Hills and Valley technique, for example, needs to be processed in hot water, with detergent, and dried in a hot dryer twice—regardless of the care instructions on the fabric.

Once the garment is finished, however, you must handle it as a fine washable. Dry clean or hand wash your creation. Don't launder in hot water or a hot dryer.

4. Press the fabric rectangle if it's wrinkled. Compare this processed piece of fabric to the outline traced on the paper. This shows you the amount that the fabric shrank.

5. Measure the amount of fabric yardage you need for your pattern pieces without allowing for shrinkage. Finding this information could be as simple as referring to the yardage on your pattern envelope.

6. Since you're working with a 10-inch fabric length, it's easy to calculate the shrinkage and yardage for your garment. The amount of shrinkage directly translates to a percentage. For example, losing 1 inch of fabric length in 10 inches means you lost $\frac{1}{10}$, or 10%, of the length. Add 100 to the percentage. Now multiply your yardage from Step 5 by this new percentage. This is the total length of yardage that you need to buy. Here's an example:
- A pattern calls for 4 yards
- The fabric shrinks 10%
- 4 x 110% = 4.4
- 4.4 yards x 36 = 158.4 inches, or just less than 4½ yards

7. There's generally less shrinkage on the crosswise grain, which is why a 5-inch width is enough for this test. Crinkled or textured fabrics are the exceptions to this rule. Use a 10 inch width when testing these types of fabrics. To calculate shrinkage, multiply the crosswise grain shrinkage on your test swatch as follows:

- By 2 to find out the amount lost every 10 inches, which can give you a percent like the lengthwise calculation above.

Or

- By 7.2 to find out the amount lost on 36-inch wide fabric.

- By 9 to find out the amount lost on 45-inch wide fabric.

- By 12 to find out the amount lost on 60-inch wide fabric.

You may find a gorgeous garment in a boutique, but it will be surpassed by a garment that has Grate Detailing. The treatment is so unusual that only a home sewer can make it, and the effect is so stylish that people will assume it came from a trendy shop. You'll also have an entertaining story about its creation.

Grate Detailing

Did you guess that the waistband texturizing on the dress to the left was made with a food grater and some fusible interfacing?

I arrived at the Grate Detailing process while making a dress. I wanted to add a small amount of interest at the waist. The challenge was finding a texturizing technique that wouldn't detract from the beautiful hand-dyed fabric. I needed an interfaced, soft, look. A food grater, hanging on a wall in my studio, caught my eye.

With a bit of experimenting, I discovered that I could make soft wrinkles by poking fabric into the holes in the grater. To make them permanent I just fused interfacing to the wrong side.

The strangest tools can help you create unique surfaces. You can use these textured pieces to add interest anywhere a garment calls for an interfaced fabric shape.

The size of your kitchen utensil limits the size of the piece you can do with this technique, so it's probably better to use the finished fabric as a decorative accent. If a garment can handle the weight of the interfacing, you certainly could make a large piece. It just requires moving the fabric around the grater more frequently.

This technique could also be used with decorative stitching over it, or as an appliqué.

Supplies

Flat, metal surface with holes (see page 56)

Permanent-fuse interfacing*

Stuff–It II, chopstick, or blunt end of pencil

Suitable Fabric

Lightweight, soft fabrics are easiest to work with, but you can use something a bit heavier. Soft silks, poly/silkies, sand-washed rayons, rayon challis, and lightweight Tencel all work well.

* Using an interfacing that's a permanent-fuse is critical so that it won't loosen when washed. Choose interfacing that gives the finished fabric the correct weight and hand for its intended use.

Texturizing the Surface

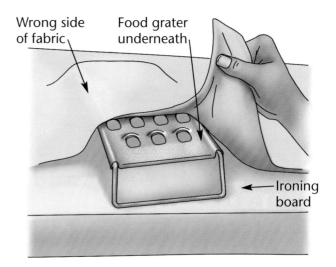

Wrong side of fabric

Food grater underneath

Ironing board

The texturizing process is simple, with plenty of room for experimenting. Simply push the fabric into some, or all, of the holes in the food grater and then fuse interfacing to the wrong side to secure the bumps. You can vary the look by pushing larger or smaller amounts of fabric into the holes.

1. It's easiest to work at an ironing board. Place the grater, legs down, on the ironing board.

2. Place your fabric, with the right side down, on top of the grater.

Lyla's Notion   Kitchen Utensils

When teaching the Grate Detailing technique, I ask students to bring a metal kitchen utensil that's flat and has holes. It is fun to see what they come up with.

Pizza pans, meat and cooling racks, food mashers, even a wire wall rack, have all made appearances. One of my favorite effects came from an unusual food masher. The student pushed fabric deep into every one of the small holes to create a finished fabric that looked like a dimensional flower.

When selecting your notion, it's best to choose one with holes that are less than ¾-inch wide, spaced far enough apart (½ to 1 inch) to hold the fabric while you work. My favorite size of hole is ¼ to ½ inch in diameter, but I never avoid trying other types of fabric and hole combinations.

Testing the hole size with the fabric is an important part of the creative process. Each tool that you find may change the rules, so it's important to experiment.

I keep the grater (shown at right) close as a remembrance of my great

A tool doesn't have to come in a package labeled "sewing supplies" to be a superb addition to your stash. The strangest items make great texturizing tools. Take a stroll around your kitchen and see what triggers your imagination.

uncle's endearing ways. He bought the grater, which was too worn to cut a thing, for a nickel at a garage sale. It still had 5 cents marked on it when he gave it to me. Uncle Harry was always proud of his bargains. His influence led me to look for coins on the ground. To this day I don't walk across a parking lot or sidewalk without keeping my eye out for a coin.

3. Use the Stuff–It II, chopstick or the blunt end of a pencil to push the fabric into the holes. It's easiest to start in the center, and slowly work out from there. Take care not to pull fabric out of the previous holes as you work. It isn't necessary to use every hole.

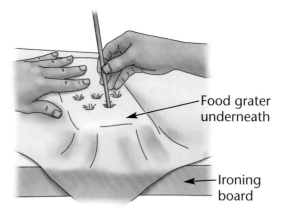

Food grater underneath

Ironing board

Securing the Texture

A fusible backing secures the fabric bubbles that you're making. The finished effect doesn't have round bumps because the last step of this process is pressing the fabric on a flat surface. This creates the random surface pattern.

1. Set the iron for steam. Place the fusible interfacing, resin side down, on top of the stuffed fabric. Tack-fuse the interfacing in position by lightly touching the surface with the iron. (A metal utensil won't melt or burn, but it may get hot. Be careful.)

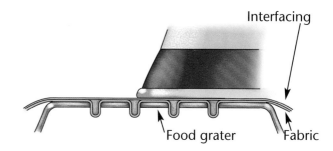

Interfacing

Food grater   Fabric

2. Remove the fabric from the grater. Reposition a new section of fabric, still right side down, on the grater's surface. Repeat the stuffing and fusing process until your textured piece is large enough for the pattern piece.

3. Fusible interfacing needs steam, heat, and pressure to permanently attach it to fabric. Check the manufacturer's instructions and follow them carefully. Since the texture isn't stitched, it's crucial that the interfacing stay in place for the life of the garment.

(in)spiration point

a modern shape gives new life to a traditional method for adding interest to a garment. One of the simplest ways to embellish a garment is using a complementary fabric for an entire garment piece. For the vest at right, I used the opposite side of the reversible denim fabric for one of the fronts. Blue decorative stitching visually links the front. It isn't much of a stretch to imagine one front of the asymmetrical vest embellished with Grate Detailing.

Lyla's Vest

The unconventional use of a gathering foot creates a coordinating fabric accent for any garment. Working with a print is especially fun because the condensed print enhances the Gathered Texture. The boutique look is achieved by making parallel rows of straight or decorative stitches while using a gathering presser foot.

Gathered Texture

Big Shirt Collection

Gathered Texture came into being when I owned a sewing machine dealership. Every month I had to come up with a new way to use a presser foot, for a sewing club that I sponsored. This wasn't a chore, because I enjoyed playing with all of the sewing machines in the store. Solving puzzles—finding interesting new techniques for all of the feet—was such a pleasure.

Join my former students; expand your stitching repertoire beyond ruffles made with a gathering presser foot.

As I said earlier in this book, one of the ways that creative sewing is inspired is by looking beyond the intended use of a notion or tool. In this case, I take advantage of the gathering capability of a specialized sewing machine presser foot, using only a single layer of fabric and continuing after the first row, where most people stop. Simple as that.

Gathering parallel rows creates a dense, all-over texture on a piece of fabric. As you gather printed fabric, the colors condense to totally change the look of the piece. This is a great way to create a coordinating fabric. It also increases the fabric density one to one-and-a-half times.

The finished effect looks great as a yoke, pocket, or cuff. I consider Gathered Texture an accent, but this doesn't have to be the case. It could be used for the entire front of a jacket.

Supplies

Chalk or tracing wheel

Gathering presser foot*

Interfacing (optional)

Quilter's guide-bar (optional)

Regular sewing thread, contrast or matching

* It's best if the needle opening on the gathering foot is an oval, to accommodate a zigzag or decorative stitch.

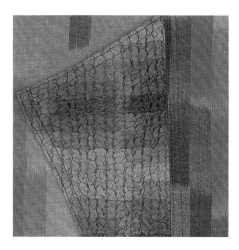

The stitching on this accent piece is serpentine, elongated for a softer curve. A similar effect is possible with a lengthened 3-step zigzag stitch. The featured fabric is a medium-weight ikat cotton. The nicest gathered texture is achieved with light- to medium-weight fabrics. Material that's too heavy is difficult to gather, and ends up fairly heavy and bulky.

Planning the Stitching

Stitch length, type of stitch, tension, and application of interfacing . . . many factors influence the finished effect. I like to experiment with a piece of fabric before working on yardage that's big enough for a pattern piece.

1. Attach a gathering foot to your machine. Set the machine for a straight stitch or else sew various forward motion decorative stitches on a fabric scrap to help you select an attractive one for the work. The serpentine stitch, also known as the mending stitch or sewn-out zigzag, is effective.

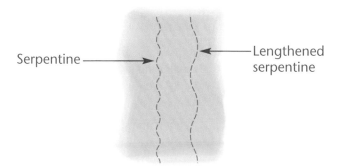

Serpentine ⟶   ⟵ Lengthened serpentine

2. Again working on a fabric scrap, lengthen the stitch and increase the upper tension. The weight of the fabric has a large bearing on the size of the adjustment you need to make. I adjust the length of the serpentine stitch until it has a soft curve. Most fabrics work well with a stitch length of 2 to 3. Adjust the stitch length first, then adjust the tension for more gathering.

3. You may want to interface the back of the textured garment piece. This can totally change the look of the fabric so, again, it's important to experiment. On a fabric scrap, sew several rows of parallel stitching about a presser foot width apart. Fuse interfacing to the wrong side of half the sample. Evaluate when cool.

Sewing the Yardage

Now it's time to gather the yardage. When finished, cut the garment pieces from the fabric.

1. Sew the first line of stitching until the row is longer than the pattern piece. I keep the pattern piece near the machine for a quick comparison.

2. Once your first row is in place, don't break the threads. It's easier to turn the fabric and stitch back to make a second row that's one presser foot width from the first. If you don't like this spacing, follow chalk lines placed at the desired width on the right side of the fabric. An alternative to chalk is a quilter's guide-bar.

3. Continue adding parallel rows of stitching, until the fabric is wide enough for your pattern piece.

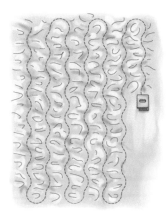

4. Interface the wrong side of the yardage, if desired.

5. Position the pattern piece on the fabric with the grainlines matching. The stitching can go in any direction. If you used a stitch length shorter than 2 simply cut out the pattern piece. Texturizing with a longer length may allow the stitch to unravel. Use chalk or a fabric marker to trace the pattern piece cutting lines on to the texturized fabric. Straight stitch around the garment shape just inside the cutting lines. This prevents the gathers from releasing when the fabric is cut. Cut out the garment piece and assemble.

FAQ FREQUENTLY ASKED QUESTION

Isn't it difficult to stitch subsequent rows because the fabric to the left is gathered and the space between the rows is so small?

It seems it would be difficult. But the answer is, "Not at all." The foot magically tucks in all the extra fabric as you sew, and it requires no action on your part.

Lyla's Notion   Gathering Foot

A gathering foot performs two actions in a single step. During the sewing process, it draws in one layer of fabric while attaching it to a second, flat, piece. The material that you want to stay flat feeds through the slot near the top of the foot. Underneath the presser foot, the other piece of fabric is gathering as you sew.

The gathering foot is designed so that pressure is intermittently released between the presser foot and the garment fabric. Whenever the pressure is released, puckers form. The effect is similar to you trying to sew while a regular presser foot is raised.

The first time that I used a gathering presser foot, I just hooked it up and started sewing on a single layer of fabric. When I switched to two layers at once, the challenge was at hand. I was now trying to simultaneously guide two fabric layers, one of which was jumping around.

Practice makes perfect. While developing my skills, I discovered the way that the fabric is held makes a big difference. Try holding the top, flat layer of fabric (the one that goes through the opening in the foot) in your left hand. Guide the fabric to the right to make sure that it stays in

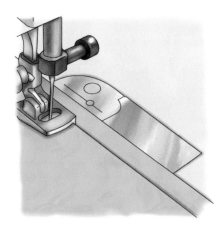

This presser foot gathers a strip of fabric, like a ruffle, at the same time that it's attached to a flat piece, such as a pillow. Mastering the foot for this purpose isn't easy. Each brand has a slightly different version of the foot, but the results are similar.

the opening in the foot. If the fabric slides too far to the left, it falls out of the opening. Your right hand holds the ruffle or gathered strip. It's important to hold the fabric gently. If it's taut, you prevent the fabric from gathering. Keep the raw edge of the ruffled strip along one of the seamline markings on the throat plate. I use the $\frac{5}{8}$-inch mark since that's what I'm used to using.

This technique requires only one layer of fabric under the foot, making it an easy way to get used to using the gathering foot before advancing to two layers for another application. Light- to medium-weight fabrics gather easily without many adjustments. The heavier the fabric, the more adjustments you need to make.

Detailing unifies a jacket and pants set. Basic pintucks are given definition by a length of cord that's worked into the wrong side of each pintuck. The cord is wrapped in the fabric and trapped by a line of double needle stitching that straddles the cord and closes the underside of the fabric fold.

Random Corded Pintucks

Kinsey Jacket

Pintucks are very structured, often frilly, and totally wrong for my fashion style. Or so I thought. I have liked the effect of pintucks for many years, yet I couldn't visualize the detailing on anything I would wear. Then a fabric came along that begged for a special treatment. It was a hand dyed piece with color changes that I wanted to emphasize. The solution was pintucks worked around these areas.

This was a breakthrough because I learned to think about pintuck applications in a new way. I then started applying pintucks to plain fabric to create coordinating pieces for garments.

To create a substantial pintuck on a medium- to heavyweight fabric, I like to insert cord. This not only defines the pintuck and gives it an attractive, round ridge, but it ensures that the pintuck remains in place.

Many garment pieces are suitable for pintucks. Apply them to an appliqué, lapel, pocket, or sleeve, for example. The outfit shown above has rows on the lapel and lower leg to draw the viewer's eye along a slimming vertical line. You can use matching or contrasting thread to further develop the look.

Supplies

Chalk

Cord guide, manufacturer's version or home-made (see page 62)

Cord or gimp

Double needle, 2.0 or 2.5 width*

Fusible or sew-in interfacing (see the FAQ on page 64)

Pintuck foot*

Small straw, 1/16- to 1/8-inch wide (optional, for the home-made cord guide)

*Choose a double needle size and width that's suitable for your pintuck presser foot and the type and weight of the fabric. Your machine manual probably offers suggestions. If you don't have a pintuck foot, try a cording foot. Both have a groove centered on the underside that's aligned with the needle. A decorative or satin stitch foot also works, because both have a raised area at the back of the foot, to accommodate a thread buildup.

Suitable Cord

Look for a stable, round cord that fits between the double needles. Pearl cotton, round and firm decorative serger threads, and some yarns work. Whatever your choice, make sure that the cord is colorfast and pre-shrunk. I buy the cord I want, then try a couple of needle sizes to see what works best.

The color of the cord doesn't matter, as long as the color doesn't show through the fabric. You can use a color for subtle shading with a lightweight, light-color fabric. On a finished pintuck, for example, an orange cord looks peach and a red cord appears pinkish. Colorfast thread is particularly important when experimenting with color.

Selecting a Cord Guide

A pintuck is made with the fabric right side up, so the cord isn't visible when stitching. You need a way to direct the cord along the underside of the fabric.

Many sewing machine companies have guides for their models. The appearance and manner that a guide operates can vary by manufacturer.

One type of guide simply snaps on to the throat plate on the sewing machine. The cord runs through the guide, ending up exactly under the center of the needle position, so it's automatically caught in the stitching.

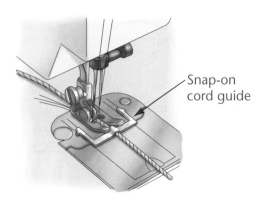

Snap-on cord guide

Some machines have a hole in the regular throat plate. The cord feeds through the hole from the underside and then extends across the top of the throat plate, centered under the needle position.

FAQ FREQUENTLY ASKED QUESTION

Can a cording presser foot hold the cord in position for random corded pintucks?

No. The cording foot guides cord on top of the fabric. The cord needs to be underneath the fabric to stitch a corded pintuck.

Making a Cord Guide

You can make a guide for cord if your machine doesn't have one, or the cord is too large to slip freely through the guide that you have.

1. Cut a ⅜-inch length from a small straw.

2. Tape a piece of straw to the machine's throat plate, directly in front of the needle hole. The distance between the end of the straw and the front of the presser foot doesn't matter, as long as the straw doesn't touch the presser foot.

3. Run the cord through the straw. The cord should feed under the presser foot, on top of the throat plate, and between the center of the needles.

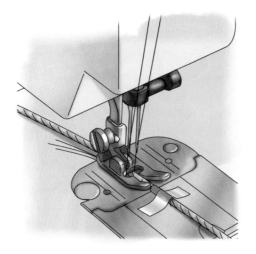

Setting Up the Machine

The cord ends up on the wrong side of the fabric, wrapped in the fabric fold and trapped by the line of stitching that closes the fold. From the wrong side, the line of stitched bobbin thread zigzags back and forth to secure both of the needle threads.

1. Install the double needle, switch the presser foot, and add the cord guide. Thread the needles.

2. Place a long piece of cord in your lap. Don't cut it into shorter pieces to match the garment piece. Insert one end of the cord through the guide. The cord needs to move freely through the guide without a lot of room. If there's too much room, the cord may slide out of position.

Lyla's Notion   Pintuck Presser Foot

This presser foot is designed to simplify the placement of parallel rows of pintucks. Grooves on the underside of the foot accommodate the columns of raised fabric that are created during stitching. The foot works by channeling the pintucks so that the fabric moves freely. If you make a pintuck with a flat-bottom presser foot the results won't be nearly as nice. The fabric could bunch in front of the foot because the raised surface has nowhere to go. Or the fabric could slip as the feed dogs move the fabric away from the stitching area that's underneath the needle.

The first pintuck is directed into one of the presser foot grooves as the second row is stitched. Then, for the next row, the first and second pintucks both ride under the presser foot. You continue filling the grooves in this manner. The guidance that this presser foot offers makes it easy to create perfectly parallel rows of stitching.

Pintuck presser feet vary from one manufacturer to the next. Consequently, some double needle widths may work better with your pintuck presser foot. Check your sewing machine manual for suggestions for suitable needle dimensions. If in doubt, place your double needle in the grooves on the bottom of the pintuck foot. The needles should be centered in the grooves.

Presser foot courtesy of Viking Husqvarna Sewing Machine

The number of grooves on the underside of a pintuck foot can vary. Choose one with enough channels that best suits your needs. If you plan to make numerous parallel rows, with the pintucks very close together, opt for a foot that has more grooves. Widely spaced, single rows of random pintucks use only the center groove.

3. Place a scrap of garment fabric, right side up, on the sewing machine so that it's on top of the cord and under the presser foot. Set your machine for a straight stitch. Hold the cord and threads behind the needle and sew the length of the scrap. Remove the fabric from the machine and then cut the cord, letting the end extend just past the fabric edge. You trim this after joining the garment pieces.

4. Inspect the pintuck. The cord should be trapped inside the fabric fold. If it isn't, switch to a smaller guide. Ideally, the bobbin thread draws together the underside of the pintuck. Adjust the needle tensions, if necessary. The height of a pintuck can be manipulated by adjusting the upper tension on your machine. For a taller pintuck, tighten the tension. For a lower pintuck, loosen the tension.

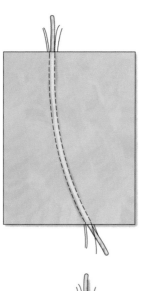

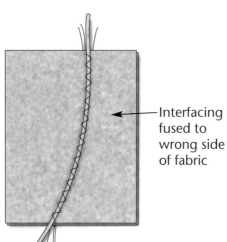

Interfacing fused to wrong side of fabric

Preparing the Garment Piece

Pintucks draw up fabric, which changes the size and shape of a garment piece. I was a math teacher, so calculating the fabric loss isn't a problem. But there's an easier way to deal with this challenge.

1. Decide the area of the garment you are pintucking. Place the corresponding pattern piece on the fabric. Chalk the pattern piece cutting lines on the fabric. Draw another set of lines about 3 or 4 inches from the cutting lines. Cut out the piece along the outermost lines. This gives you a fabric size that's easy to manipulate on the machine. The outer lines give you a general idea where you are on the pattern piece. This is helpful when you're trying to create mirror images, like on matching lapels. You can use the excess fabric, outside the cutting lines, to taper the stitching to a point and turn the stitching line for the next row. You also have plenty of fabric to accommodate the fabric that's drawn in by the pintucks.

2. If using fusible interfacing, apply it to the wrong side of the fabric piece.

3. Cut out the fabric shape along the outermost chalked lines.

FAQ **FREQUENTLY ASKED QUESTION**

What's the best way to choose an interfacing for this technique?

Experiment! Try making some pintucks after applying fusible interfacing to the wrong side of the fabric. (Applying a fusible after making pintucks destroys the definition in the fabric ridges.) Sew-in interfacing stabilizes the pintucked piece after the stitching is complete.

Placing the Pintucks

There aren't any rules for placing pintucks. Let go of any tendencies to work in straight, rigid lines.

1. Sew across your fabric piece in any direction. I stitched the jacket lapel on page 61 in a large, wiggly zigzag. It's difficult to start and stop the lines of stitching since you're working with 2 needle threads, a bobbin thread, and a length of cord. Instead, sew all the way across the fabric piece, turning near the edge. Sew the next row without breaking the threads.

FAQ FREQUENTLY ASKED QUESTION

Who sells small straws?

Pick up one of the straws at a coffeehouse or a latte stand. There are a great variety of sizes, so you're sure to find one that's perfect for your selected cord.

2. Chalk or place the pattern piece on the finished, pintucked fabric. (For garment pieces that need mirror images, place two pieces of stitched fabric right sides together, matching the pintucks.) Cut out the garment shape.

Pattern shape

inspiration point

a facing is a terrific spot for decorative detail. Rather than working only horizontal rows, I added vertical pintucks to create interesting box shapes. Embellish the garment piece and then stitch the right side of the facing to the wrong side of the vest. Now fold the facing to the outside and edge stitch the loose side in position.

The visual and tactile texture on the front panels of this jacket create slimming vertical lines in an otherwise traditional garment. The complex effect is a dynamite combination of interesting techniques that are featured earlier in this section. If you love making corded pintucks and working with a gathering stitch, this is going to be your favorite technique.

Gathered Pintucks

Galleria Jacket

O ne day I wondered what would happen if I combined some of my favorite techniques. Curiosity urged me on, and the results are fabulous. The finished fabric has a beautiful weight. So many people asked me how I created the texture that I had to develop these instructions.

The process builds on Random Corded Pintucks and Gathered Texture, both featured earlier in this chapter. Using a double needle, the texturizing is created by straight stitching parallel lines of elastic-corded pintucks while feeding the fabric under a gathering presser foot.

By using elastic thread to cord the pintucks, you texturize and build slight stretch into any piece of fabric. The resulting stretch is in the direction of the stitching.

If you want two-way stretch, then all you have to do is sew vertical and horizontal lines on the fabric.

It's a good idea to make test samples and experiment with all techniques. This is particularly important for a technique like Gathered Pintucks.

Set aside some time to play with fabric weights, needle size, and tension. Your tests will help you come up with a pleasing effect and also master the skills needed to control the stitching process.

Supplies

Cord guide, manufacturer's version or home-made (see page 62)

Decorative or regular sewing thread

Double needle, about 2.0/80

Elastic thread

Gathering foot with an oval (zigzag) needle hole

Small straw (optional, for home-made cord guide)

Suitable Thread, Fabric, and Needle

Let the fabric type guide your needle selection. The elastic thread should fill the space between the needles during pintucking. Light- to medium-weight wovens and knits look great. Rayon challis is one of my favorite choices. In general, the heavier the fabric, the farther apart you can place the rows of stitching for nice results. Use regular or decorative thread that doesn't break easily.

Preparing the Machine

It's best to use a gathering presser foot with an oval needle hole that's wide enough for a zigzag stitch. The two sides of the double needle won't fit through a smaller opening.

1. Attach the gathering presser foot. Install the double needle and set the machine for a straight stitch. Adjust the needle tension to create a slight gather. The tighter the upper tension on your machine, the more the fabric gathers.

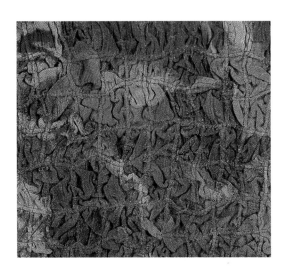

This is a close-up of a skirt yoke. I stitched across one side of the fabric, leaving the majority of the length flat. At the end of each row, I pivoted the work and then stitched the next line. This finished the yoke bottom, where the flat fabric falls below the textured fabric, without a seam.

2. Attach the cord guide to the machine. (See page 62 for instructions to make a cord guide.) Thread the double needles with regular or decorative thread, and put regular thread on the bobbin.

3. Run the elastic thread through the guide so that it feeds under the presser foot and between the needles. Pull the end of the cord out the back of the machine, behind the presser foot.

FREQUENTLY ASKED QUESTION

Why not use elastic thread in the bobbin?

It's much simpler to treat the elastic thread as cord. As anyone who has tried stitching with an elastic-filled bobbin can attest, you won't stitch very far before reloading. Elastic thread is so bulky that a bobbin only holds enough to sew a couple rows. Who wants to spend a lot of time winding bobbins? This technique gives similar results in less time with less frustration. If that isn't enough, keep in mind that it's difficult to use the gathering foot with elastic thread in the bobbin and, if you did, the interesting ridges would be missing.

Stitching the Fabric

As in Gathered Texture, we create a piece of fabric large enough for the pattern piece.

1. Start with a piece of fabric that's about 25% larger than the pattern piece. For example, if you need 20 inches of texturized fabric, start with a piece that's 25-inches wide. (You only cut the garment piece from the fabric after texturizing the material.)

2. Place the fabric, right side up, on the sewing machine bed. The elastic thread is underneath. (Don't worry if the elastic isn't caught in every stitch. The overall effect won't be ruined.)

3. Hold the threads behind the machine and start sewing at one fabric edge. Place your hands on the fabric, and wiggle it as you stitch. Sew a line to the opposite side of the fabric. Don't stretch the elastic. It's difficult to stitch a straight line while the gathering foot is puckering the fabric and the elastic is pulling on it. You need a lot of concentration because the fabric is hopping around under the presser foot. So stop trying. Besides, straight lines and squares aren't nearly as interesting as the odd shapes formed with crooked lines of stitching.

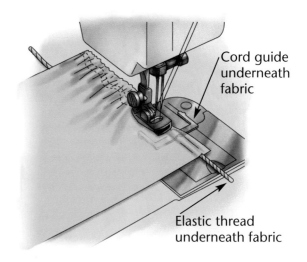

Cord guide underneath fabric

Elastic thread underneath fabric

Lyla's Notion   ## Double Needle

A double needle is commonly used for topstitching, pintucks, and other decorative stitches.

Two needles extend from a single shank, so that you can make two evenly spaced, parallel lines of stitching in a single pass. Since there's a single length of thread coming from the bobbin, it links with both needle threads to form a zigzag on the underside of the stitch.

There are many sizes and types of double needles. The designation on the package shows several things. For example, 2.5/75 stretch means the size 75 needles are spaced 2.5 mm apart and they're designed to sew on knit fabrics.

Following a few simple steps when threading your double needle can save you the frustration of tangled and broken threads. Place the spools on your machine so the thread feeds off the spools in opposite directions. As you thread your machine, keep the two strands separate. Place one thread on each side of the tension disk. If there's a single thread guide just before the needle, use it for one of the threads. Leave the second thread out of the guide.

Double needles can be used on any sewing machine that's capable of making a zigzag stitch. You must, however, ensure that the presser foot mounted on the machine has a needle hole wide enough to accommodate the two needles.

As you start to sew, be sure to hold the threads. This is one of the few times when you want to stick to a rule!

Double needles may be used with a straight, decorative, or pattern stitch. Your only limitations are the width of the double needle, openings in the machine's throat plate and presser foot, and stitch. To find the maximum pattern stitch width for any combination, subtract the width of the double needle from the stitch width. For example, if the maximum stitch width for your machine is 6 and the double needle width is 2.5, your maximum pattern stitch width is 3.5. (6-2.5=3.5)

Double needles can create a permanent ridge of fabric between the two lines of stitching. To flatten the ridge, loosen the needle tensions. To make the ridge more prominent, increase the needle tensions.

4. At the end of the stitching line, pivot the fabric and sew another row parallel to the first. My favorite results were made with a ¼- to ½-inch space between the rows. Continue stitching additional rows until the fabric is covered.

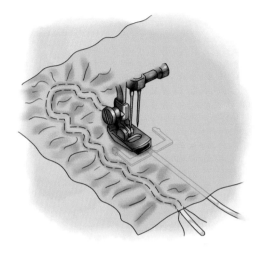

5. You can make randomly shaped squares, as shown in the photo on page 69. To do this, pivot the fabric and make more rows of stitching that are generally perpendicular to the rows created in Step 4.

FAQ FREQUENTLY ASKED QUESTION

If wiggly stitching lines look better than straight, why not use a serpentine stitch?

The double needle slams into the sides of the presser foot if a wide stitch is selected. Also, the elastic thread is less likely to end up between the needles with serpentine stitching.

Assembling the Garment

This is the simplest part of the project, because fabric that's texturized with Gathered Pintucks doesn't need special handling.

As a general rule, to maintain the quality of the give in the fabric, and to keep the softly gathered texture, don't interface the wrong side of the texturizing. The wrong side of this finished fabric isn't attractive. When I make an unlined jacket, like the one shown on page 66, I hide the wrong side. This is done by fusing a soft, stretchy interfacing to the wrong side of the texturized fabric before cutting out the pattern piece.

Cut the pattern shape from the texturized fabric. Although not necessary, to secure the ends of the cord you can trace the pattern cutting lines on to the fabric, straight stitch just inside the lines, and then cut out the garment pieces.

Be cautious about trimming seam allowances after joining the texturized pieces. I wouldn't trim any more than absolutely necessary. If close trimming is necessary, sew 2 rows of stitching on the seamline. The elastic doesn't pull out of the stitching, but could under stress.

Hems

On the black jacket shown on page 66, I hemmed the Gathered Pintuck fabric with a narrow, balanced serger stitch. Your fabric can be turned up and top-stitched, sewn by hand, or bound.

Waistbands

To duplicate my skirt yoke treatment, attach a separate, flat piece of fabric to make the elasticized waistband. As I mention in the photo caption on page 67, you don't need to make separate garment pieces for the yoke and skirt. Just make the yoke by stitching gathered pintucks to the top of the fabric. The fabric below the gathered pintucks, which isn't embellished, is the fuller portion of the skirt that's underneath the yoke. All you need to do now is make the side seams and add a closure.

Closures

Shy away from buttons. Fabrics suitable for this technique could be folded back to accommodate zippers without too much added bulk. The easiest treatment is a hidden zipper.

Annapolis Tunic and Pants

Kanisha Dress

Sassy Jacket

On The Edge

Edge treatments on garments are commonplace, although they need not be boring. You can use the edge of your garment to showcase some terrific techniques that are explained in this chapter. From a special Gathered Piping technique for a soft scalloped edge, to a simplified fold-over binding, you'll find the perfect technique for your next project. If you need a bit of guidance in creating easy—but beautiful—bound edges, read on.

I started looking at garments in an entirely new way when I launched my pattern line. Until then, I used to avoid edge finishes, particularly binding, at all costs. The techniques were too frustrating. Yet the polished effect of many treatments was perfect for my garments. I forced myself to learn more.

First came easier ways to apply binding, then an exploration of materials that can replace a bias fabric strip and, finally, some shorter processes. Now binding is one of my favorite ways to finish garments.

I hope that you, too, will enjoy binding once you try the techniques on the following pages.

But this chapter is about more than binding. It's also about designer finishes such as Reversible Serging. (See page 81.) This is where the same serger edge finish can make a garment totally reversible. Whether used to make sweats or a jacket, you'll love the fact that you have two garments in one by adding one simple step to the regular construction process.

After trying the featured techniques, you'll think you died and went to heaven.

Opposite sides of the same fabric offer visual contrast at the neckline of this Polar Fleece jacket. The edge finish is merely the textured, inner surface of a fabric strip that's converted into an easy-to-make, even-width binding. You can duplicate the effect with any non-fraying fabric.

Convertible Jacket

Fray-Free & Easy Binding

By using water-soluble thread and a paper-backed fusible webbing in combination with any non-raveling fabric, you can create a quick and easy fold-over trim. The goof-proof procedure gives you an even-width binding along the entire edge.

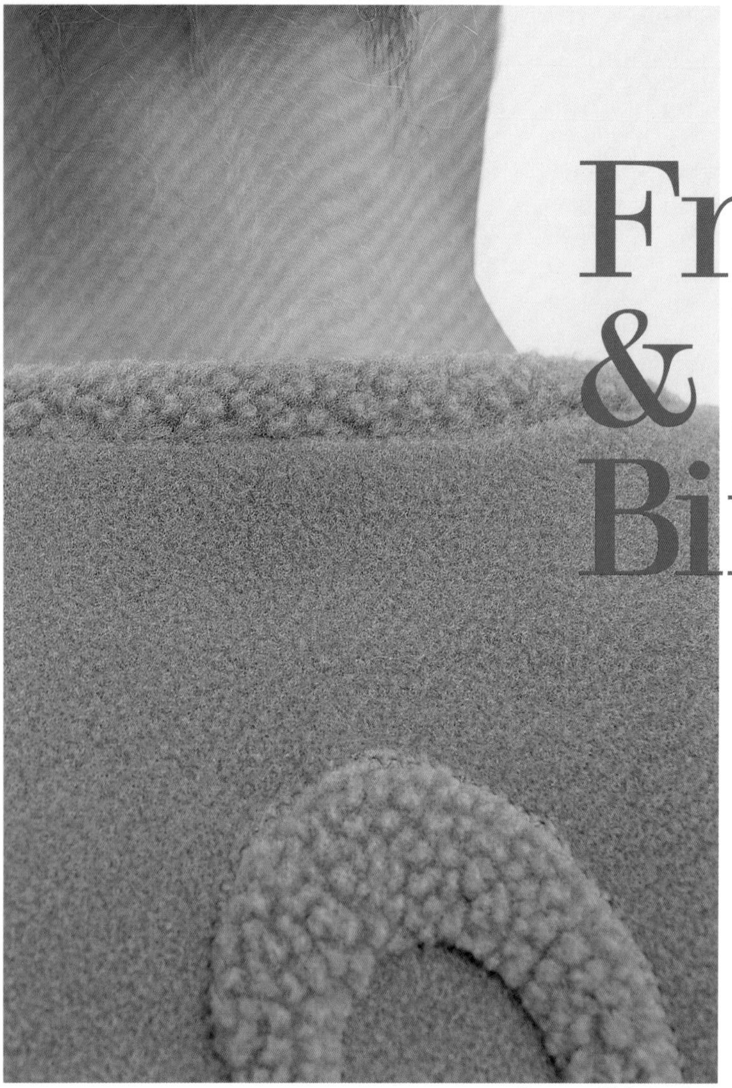

This is a great technique for a binding that's made from a fleece fabric.

As is often the case, the Fray-Free & Easy Binding evolved from a problem-solving session. I needed an attractive finish for the edges of garments that featured sculpted fleece designs. (See Sculpted Appliqué on page 34.) On previous occasions, I tried folding a strip of non-raveling fabric over the edge and then simply stitched it in place. As you can imagine, it was difficult to make the edges meet at precisely the same location on the inside and outside of the garment; there were spots where the edge or edges didn't catch in the stitching. I wasn't at all satisfied with the results. What I needed was a placement line that would be visible on both sides of the fabric. It was also important to be able to fuse the binding in place without crushing the binding.

That's when I stumbled across the process that evolved into the Fray-Free & Easy Binding technique. Now I can successfully bind with a wide array of fabrics that were formerly off limits.

Supplies

Chalk marking pencil (optional)

Edge stitch presser foot (optional)

Transparent or matching all-purpose thread

Ultra-Soft Double-Sided Fusible (UsDsF, a paper-backed fusible webbing)

Water bottle with spray nozzle

Water-soluble thread

Suitable Fabric

Initially developed for felted and plush non-woven fabrics, any fabric that doesn't fray along a cut edge can be used. I've worked successfully with stable knits that have a tight loop construction, UltraSuede, Facile, Polar Fleece, boiled or felted wool, and stable knits. Some Lycra knits are also suitable. Look for the heavy, closely knit Lycra that doesn't fray and remains flat when edge stitched.

Establishing the Binding Width

Don't automatically make the binding on your garments a standard width.

As a rule of thumb, the heavier or bulkier the fabric, the wider the binding. Much of the determination of width, however, is personal preference. That's why the following testing method is the easiest way to see what I like. Keep in mind that the UsDsF is ³⁄₈-inch wide. If you opt for a binding width narrower than that, you need to trim the UsDsF.

1. On the garment (or on a piece of the garment fabric) make several rows of basting ³⁄₈ inch, ½ inch, and ⁵⁄₈ inch from the edge.

2. Cut a 5-inch long, 1½-inch wide sample of the binding fabric.

3. Place your binding sample on the ½ inch basting line. Join the pieces with pins placed parallel—and as close as possible—to the edge of the binding.

4. Fold the excess binding over the edge to the wrong side, pin it in place, and assess the appearance. If it's a little too narrow, try again with the binding pinned at the basting line farthest from the edge. If it looks a little too wide, try the ³⁄₈-inch basting line.

5. Once you have decided on the width, pin- or chalk-mark on the wrong side of the binding where it matches the basting on the garment.

Versa Jacket

A black stable knit is the perfect companion for the burn-out fabric used to make this lightweight jacket. The cut edges of a stable knit won't ravel or curl so you can edge stitch the raw edge of the binding in position in the final step. The edge of a plush fabric binding like fleece is secured with zigzag stitches.

6. Cut away the excess binding fabric past the pin- or chalk-mark. Measure the width of the trimmed binding strip. Cut the binding strips to this width. Remove the sample binding from the garment.

Preparing the Pieces

A simple line of stitching on the garment edge guides the placement of the binding. Since the stitching guide is visible on the right and wrong sides of the fabric, the binding ends up in exactly the same location on both sides of the garment.

1. Along the crosswise grain, cut the binding fabric into strips of the desired width and length.

2. Join the strips end-to-end until you have a piece that's long enough to cover the entire edge. The simplest way to join the ends is to straight stitch across the short edges using a ¼ inch seam allowance.

3. Fuse UsDsF, paper side up, on the wrong side of both long edges of the binding. Finger-press, using steam, if the binding is a crushable fabric. Otherwise, fuse by pressing an iron to the paper surface.

4. Assemble the garment pieces to the point where the binding is attached.

5. Set your sewing machine for a long (4 mm) stitch length. Place water-soluble thread in the needle and in the bobbin.

6. Insert the garment edge under the presser foot so that you can make a line of straight stitching the same distance from the edge as the desired finished width of the binding. Sew around the entire garment edge.

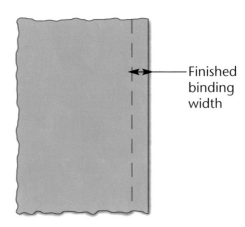

Finished binding width

Lyla's Notion
Ultra-Soft Double-Sided Fusible

All you need is an iron and Ultra-Soft Double-Sided Fusible (UsDsF) to hem fine fabrics, control knit hems, create fusible trim, position zippers, match plaids and stripes, tack facings, and stabilize buttonholes. I'm sure there are even more uses because UsDsF can be used as a stabilizer or bonding agent wherever two pieces of fabric need to be permanently joined.

UsDsF is virtually impossible to detect after application. Unlike some products, it won't leave a sticky residue on a sewing machine needle when you sew through it. However, UsDsF does have its limits. It may pull loose at the garment stress points, so avoid applying UsDsF to these areas or reinforce the UsDsF application with stitching.

Here's how you apply the product. Press the paper-backed adhesive, paper side up, to the wrong side of the fabric with a steam or dry iron. It takes very little heat and pressure to fuse UsDsF to fabric. This is specially helpful when working with a crushable fabric. You can simply steam on the paper side of the tape—using little or no pressure—remove the iron, and then finger-press.

A two-in-one product, UsDsF is both a glue and a stabilizer. You can use it wherever two pieces of fabric need to be permanently joined. It's also great for stabilizing a fabric for stitching. All you have to do is fuse the UsDsF to one of the fabrics.

Peel off the paper and place the adhesive-coated fabric against the second piece of fabric. Obtain a permanent bond by pressing with steam for 6 to 10 seconds. Fusing time varies by fabric type, thickness, and iron temperature. Test a sample of the fabric before starting your project.

Dry-clean or wash and dry your finished project with cool settings—heat can soften and release the adhesive, although you can re-fuse it, if necessary.

Attaching Binding

Fusible webbing holds the front and back of the binding in position until you secure the edges of both sides with a single line of stitching.

1. Remove the UsDsF paper from one lengthwise edge. Press this edge, fusible side down, on the right side of the garment. As you position the binding, align the raw lengthwise edge with the straight stitching.

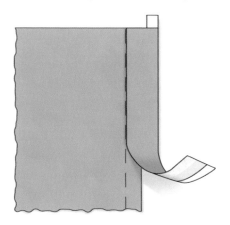

2. Without pressing the opposite side, fuse the positioned half. Steam and finger-press.

3. Remove the paper backing from the remaining side. With the garment wrong side up, wrap the binding around the edge to the water-soluble stitching line. Fuse.

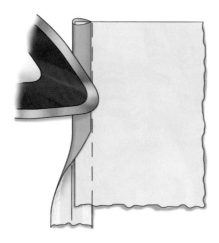

4. Plush fabrics look best with a 2 mm zigzag stitch and transparent thread. Center the stitch over the binding edge. I prefer a straight stitch for Lycra or other stable knit bindings. Use a longer stitch (about 3 mm) ⅛ inch inside the cut edge of the binding. Sew from the right side.

Flat fabric

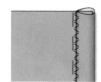

Plush fabric

---

inspiration point

Why avoid fabric that ravels? You can take advantage of the loose weave to create a fringed trim or binding. Merely fringe one—or both—lengthwise edges of a fabric strip and adapt the Fray-Free & Easy Binding instructions. Position the water-soluble thread stitching guideline on the garment so that it's just beyond the outer edge of the fringe.

Attach fringed trim with decorative thread and an interesting stitch that's centered down the length of the strip. The fringed binding and trim in the jacket shown at right were attached with Halo Thread.

Sassy Jacket

A jacket gets an "edge" with textural binding. Applying rib knit fabric strips requires a technique that won't damage the fabric's loft or volume. A strip of fusible webbing solves the problem, simplifies the application process, and makes it easier to achieve an even-width along the entire edge. Only a practiced eye will notice that there's a right side.

Double Fold Binding

LaConner Jacket

I enjoy texture and volume, so it was only a matter of time before I tried attaching crushable, or napped fabric bindings to garment edges.

These materials pose a few challenges, because you don't want to ruin the binding fabric when attaching it to the garment edge. Pressing, for example, should be minimized so that the fabric retains its loft. By experimenting, I discovered that using fusible webbing on one of the long binding edges solved the problem. This also means that I no longer have to press under a lengthwise edge before attaching the second, opposite edge to the garment.

This simple binding technique is less stressful than making a turned-edge, fold-over binding.

Contrasting the Double Fold Binding process with the more traditional technique, you can see that there are only a few small changes, but these make a world of difference. For starters, you use a contrast color thread in the bobbin when sewing the first edge of the binding to the garment. Now you have a visible placement line for positioning the opposite binding edge. The second change is adding a strip of fusible webbing to the remaining loose edge. You don't need pins and the binding won't slip.

Supplies

⅜-inch wide Ultra-Soft Double-Sided Fusible (UsDsF, a paper-backed fusible webbing)

All-purpose thread*

Edge stitch presser foot (optional)

Suitable Fabric

Almost all types can be used, from firmly woven to light- and medium-weight knits. Find a texture, color, and weight that will work with your garment. For example, a soft garment needs a fabric binding that drapes with the garment and stabilizes the edge.

*You need one spool that matches either the binding or the garment and another that contrasts with the garment.

LaConner Jacket

The Double Fold Binding was developed for this jacket. It begged for a binding but I didn't want to crush the soft wool by using a traditional binding method. The fusible thread binding technique (see Lyla's Notion on page 41) wouldn't work so it was time to experiment!

Establishing the Width

The width of the finished binding is a matter of taste. As a general rule, however, a heavy or bulky garment fabric looks best with a wider binding. Make it at least ⅜-inch wide so that it matches the width of the UsDsF. If you want narrower binding, trim the UsDsF to slightly less than—or equal to—the width of the finished binding.

1. Estimate the desired width of the finished binding. Cut a small sample strip three times the desired width plus ⅜ inch.

2. If the binding is too narrow to completely turn the UsDsF edge under before you fuse, you'll need to add more to the next test strip to give you enough fabric. If the binding is too wide, and hangs off the cut edge of the fabric at the garment edge, you need to reduce the width.

Preparing the Binding

It's just as easy to cut individual strips as it is to make continuous bias. Continuous bias works equally well.

1. Cut your garment binding to the same width as the sample binding. Cut woven fabrics on the bias and knit fabrics on the crosswise grain.

2. To make a diagonal seam, place the ends of two strips together at a right angle. Pin a diagonal seam and open the lengths to ensure that you'll end up with a straight, joined strip. Refold and sew. Trim the seam allowances and press them open.

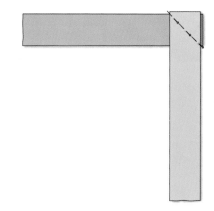

3. Continue joining binding strips until you have a suitable length.

4. Press a strip of UsDsF to the right side of the binding, aligning one edge of the strip with one long edge of the binding.

Attaching Binding

Contrasting thread attaches the binding and doubles as a placement guide.

1. Assemble the garment pieces to the point where the binding is attached. Set your sewing machine for a regular stitch length. Load the bobbin with a contrasting thread.

2. Pin the edge of the binding without UsDsF to the garment, right sides together and raw edges even.

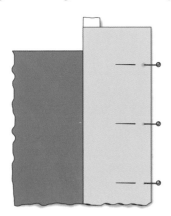

Sassy Jacket

At the point where the lapel folds to the outside of the garment (the break point), stop sewing and break the threads. Don't backstitch. Pull the threads to the wrong side and tie them off. Flip over the garment, and edge stitch with the opposite side of the binding facing up for the remainder of the jacket. Stop when you reach the opposite break point and change direction again.

3. Insert the garment edge under the presser foot so that the straight stitching will be the same distance from the edge as the desired finished width of the binding. Sew around the entire garment edge.

4. Remove the UsDsF paper. With the garment wrong side up and working on small sections, roll the loose side of the binding over the seam allowances. Turn under the loose edge so that the UsDsF is hidden.

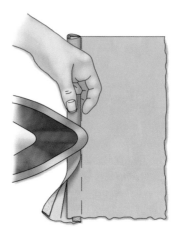

5. Place the folded edge over the contrasting stitching. Steam and finger-press the binding in position. Use minimal pressure so that you don't flatten the fabric.

6. Working from the right side, edge stitch the binding ⅛ inch from the previous seamline. The new line of stitching that you are adding secures the folded edge in position on the garment. Since the folded edge was placed over the contrasting stitching line in the previous step, your new line of stitching will be positioned perfectly.

Binding can be the focal point of a boutique-quality garment. Over-stitched binding elevates an ordinary edging to an extraordinary finish. You can enhance the decorative effect by using a thread that complements the garment. In this jacket, for example, the subtle shimmer of the hand-woven fabric is repeated in the silver thread on the binding.

Jazz It Up Binding

Versa Jacket

As is often the case with my techniques, the Jazz It Up Binding evolved out of necessity. While teaching at the Sewing and Stitchery Expo in Puyallup, Washington, I met a weaver who creates fabrics with incredible drape. Several of my patterns are a perfect match for Linda Kubik's yardage: The Versa Jacket, SophistiCoat and Zea Vest Collection have simple lines, only a few pattern pieces, and require fabric that drapes well. Linda and I had fun exchanging fabrics for patterns.

Back in my studio with my treasures, I transformed a beautiful piece of aqua-colored fabric into a Versa Jacket. Unfortunately, my test samples for the binding were disappointing. The "perfect" matching binding fabric was dull and lifeless when placed beside the jacket fabric. The metallic thread woven into the fabric every couple of inches gives it a subtle vibrancy that overwhelmed the binding. The solution, I decided, was to give the binding a little boost in this direction. Serger stitching over the narrow bound edge with a metallic thread did the trick.

The technique is simple. Instead of edge-stitching or stitching in the ditch to complete the binding, stitch over it.

Supplies

Light– to medium–weight decorative thread*

Matching serger thread

*You need a thread that's strong enough to run through the serger loopers without breaking.

Use a light- to medium-weight decorative thread. Fabric will show between the stitches, which prevents the thread from overpowering the binding. You can adapt this technique for a sewing machine by decoratively stitching over the binding. It'll take longer and you'll need a presser foot that has a channel on the bottom to accommodate the bulk of the bound edge.

1. Decide the width of the finished binding. This width should match the widest stitch on the serger.

2. Place decorative thread in the upper and lower loopers of the serger. Match the needle thread to the fabric or binding color.

3. Set the serger for a balanced 3-thread stitch that's slightly wider than the binding. Use a long stitch length so that the binding is visible underneath. Disengage the serger knives.

4. Assemble the garment. Using the Double Fold Binding instructions on page 76, attach the binding. Stop before you edge stitch it in position.

5. Serge over the bound edge so the stitching wraps around the edge. The groove on the underside of the presser foot, which accommodates thread build-up when serging, guides the bound edge.

Lyla's Notion — Halo Thread

Halo Thread has an interesting texture and is completely washable. In addition, there's a great selection of colors. The combination of fibers causes colors to flicker across the surface.

The blend also gives this acrylic fiber a soft, brushed texture. The round fibers are twisted with a flat, metallic polyester film that adds an interesting reflective quality.

Halo thread is easy to work with because you don't need to make many tension adjustments. It can't be used in a regular needle, but works very well when threaded through a topstitching needle. Used properly, the thread won't split or break when it's used for decorative stitching.

Halo thread is strong and requires almost no tension adjustments. The thread works well for a rolled hem, chain stitching, flatlocking, cover stitching, couching, bobbin stitching, and even machine quilting.

Defy conventional math. One fabric plus one serger stitch equals two wonderful edge finishes <u>and</u> one great-looking garment. The pink side of this jacket displays seams that look like conventional topstitching. Turn the jacket inside out to reveal decorative seams and the other side of the reversible fabric.

Reversible Serging

Sassy Jacket

*F*orget complex tension settings—even a beginning sewer can easily replicate the look of flatlocking or braid with this simple technique. All you need is balanced 3-thread overlocking and straight machine stitching.

The concept is simple. Serge a seam in the usual manner. Press the seam allowance to one side so that decorative thread, positioned in the upper looper, is exposed. Only one more step makes this ordinary seam extraordinary: just edge stitch the loose side of the serged seam allowance flat against the garment. Now the serged seam allowance has a decorative appearance. The opposite side, which is called Side 1 in the following instructions, looks topstitched.

Construction starts with double-sided fabric. You can purchase your own, or else create personalized fabric by combining two pieces of yardage. This isn't as difficult as it sounds. Just join two fabrics, wrong sides together, with temporary adhesive spray. Now secure the layers with randomly sewn straight, decorative, or free-motion stitching.

Supplies

All-purpose serger thread

Chalk marking pencil

Edge stitch presser foot (optional)

Heat-resistant decorative serger thread*

Matching sewing machine thread

*Just learning to use decorative threads in your serger? Keep tension adjustments to a minimum by using decorative thread that has a similar weight to regular serger thread. Halo thread, PolYarn, and variegated all-purpose threads are good choices. The serger stitching must be pressed, so don't choose a thread that melts when heated.

Cutting Out the Shapes

Choose a pattern with simple lines and minimal detail. In addition to the Sassy Jacket shown on page 84, other patterns that work well are the Asymmetrical Tunic & Skirt, SophistiCoat, Freedom Wrap, Kanisha Jacket, Ultimate Broomstick Skirt, and the single-breasted version of the LaConner Jacket. To order any of these garment patterns in the L. J. Design collection, see page 118. Unless you're willing to experiment, it's best to avoid features like tucks, pleats, and pockets.

1. Pretreat the fabric.

2. One side of the finished garment looks like it has conventional seams. Except for the hems and edges, no serging is visible. In the following instructions, this is Side 1. Decide which side of your fabric will be Side 1. The garment side that sports decorative stitching is called Side 2.

3. Fold the fabric with Side 1 on the inside and cut out the pattern shapes. When using asymmetrical pieces like the cranberry tunic on page 70 and at bottom left, cut a single layer of fabric with the right side up.

4. Label Side 1 of every garment shape.

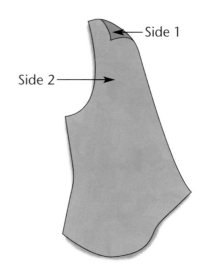

Annapolis

There are hidden treasures in this photo! The pants and top are reversible. The seams look great on both sides because I used a 3-thread serger stitch and straight machine stitching. A lettuce edge hem is created with a narrow balanced overlock serger stitch.

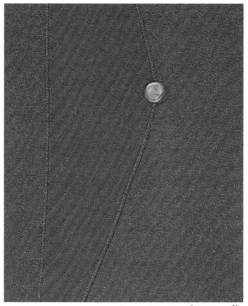

Annapolis

In the combination shown above, the fluffy side of the fleece is used for a contrasting front panel. Turn the garment inside out to reveal the opposite—equally beautiful—side of each fabric.

Preparing the Machines

Coordinate the serger and sewing machine threads to contrast or complement Sides 1 and 2 of the new garment.

1. Adjust your serger for the widest, balanced, 3-thread overlock stitch. Use only the left needle on a 3/4 thread serger. Place decorative thread in the upper looper and matching regular serger thread in the needle and lower looper.

2. Using scraps of the garment fabric, experiment with the stitch width and length. When working on a woven fabric, good coverage is important. You don't want any fabric visible between the stitches. (Try a shorter stitch length with lightweight threads.) Knit fabrics are more forgiving. You can choose a longer stitch length so the fabric shows through the thread, thus adding dimension.

3. Load the sewing machine with thread that matches the serger needle thread. Choose the bobbin thread color based on the desired effect for the topstitching on Side 1 (the side with topstitched seams).

Planning the Assembly

The position of the decorative thread on each seam allowance determines how the garment is assembled. The seam allowances are serged and then topstitched to the garment to expose the decorative thread in the upper looper.

Before joining any garment pieces, decide which direction the seam allowances will be pressed. This determines how the pieces are assembled. The decorative thread appears on the side of the seam that's face up when serged. For example, if the side seams will be pressed toward the garment back, the

front and back must be serged together with the garment front on top when you serge the seam. You'll be serging the seams in opposite directions—one side top to bottom, one side bottom to top. When the seam is pressed toward the back, the decorative thread from the upper looper is visible.

Seaming the Garment

As usual, garment details like darts and decorative stitching are finished first, then the seaming begins.

1. Make any darts. Fold the garment piece with Side 1 on the inside. Straight stitch the dart and press it down or toward the center of the garment. Still using a straight stitch, topstitch the folded edge of the loose side of the dart to the garment.

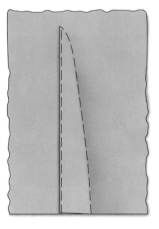

Side 2

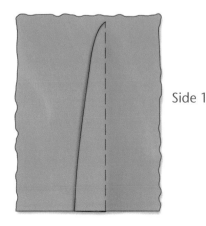

Side 1

FAQ
FREQUENTLY ASKED QUESTION

Is there a way to prevent the upper and lower layers from shifting when I start serged seams on bulky fabrics, like fleece, or on slippery fabrics, like silkies?

The beginning of a serged seam can be difficult to control, particularly when working with bulky fabrics like fleece or boiled wool. The presser foot pulls the top fabric layer forward while the bottom layer is pulled in the opposite direction by the feed dogs. To control the shifting, simply straight stitch the first ¼ inch of the seam before making the start of the serger seam.

2. To make the first seam, place Side 1 of two garment pieces together and align the raw edges.

3. At the serger, position the stacked pieces so that the needle is on the seamline (usually ⅝ inch from the raw edge). Serge together the garment pieces, letting the knives cut off any excess seam allowance.

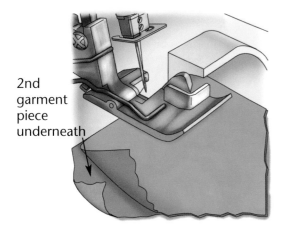

2nd garment piece underneath

4. Press the seam allowance to one side. Make sure that the decorative thread is visible. Tuck the serger chain at each end of the seamline between the seam allowance and the garment. Pin them in place until an

adjacent line of stitching secures the ends in another seam allowance.

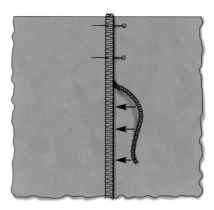

5. Edge stitch the loose side of the serged seam allowance to the garment piece. Sew back and forth over the decorative thread within the seam allowances to secure the loose serger chain.

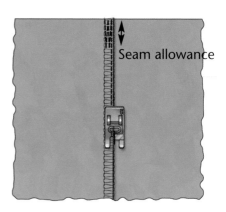

Seam allowance

6. Make the remaining garment seams following Steps 2 through 5.

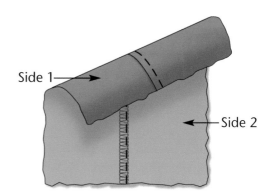

Side 1

Side 2

Defining garment edges with piping isn't a new idea, but the scalloped effect certainly is. A strip of fabric and rows of gathering stitches transform simple piping into an extraordinary edge finish. Depending on the garment, location of the detail, and choice of accent fabric, Gathered Piping looks traditional, elegant, or fun.

Gathered Piping

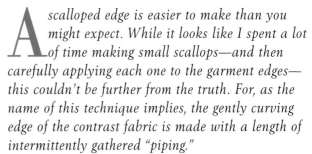

Kanisha Dress

A scalloped edge is easier to make than you might expect. While it looks like I spent a lot of time making small scallops—and then carefully applying each one to the garment edges—this couldn't be further from the truth. For, as the name of this technique implies, the gently curving edge of the contrast fabric is made with a length of intermittently gathered "piping."

You start with a fabric strip that's wider than the desired finished width. Now make evenly spaced, parallel rows of gathering across the width. (A gathering foot simplifies this process, but you can draw up a basting stitch or cord over which you zigzag stitched.) Now all that's left is folding the fabric strip in half lengthwise and attaching it to the edge with a single line of stitching.

One very important thing to remember when you plan to apply Gathered Piping is that the garment must have a facing or another garment part that covers the seam allowances and ensures the piping juts out from the edge.

On the dress above, you can see that the scalloped edge of the piping offers several benefits. Without the contrast of the soft edge and multi-color fabric, the linen dress would be rather boring. Also notice how the piping creates a flattering vertical line on the dress. This keeps the eye moving up and down, which has a slimming effect. Finally, the piping coordinates with the godet at the sides.

Supplies

Chalk marking pencil (optional)

Gathering presser foot (optional)

Temporary ink fabric marker

Water bottle with spray nozzle

Water-soluble thread

The edge of an otherwise plain garment assumes a boutique-quality finish with the addition of scallops. The piping is fast and easy to make, but looks like it took hours to perfect. Using a gathering foot is the easiest way to make the scallops on the contrast fabric, but you can produce the same effect with little more than short rows of basting stitches that are drawn up to make the gathers.

Suitable Fabric

Light- to medium-weight wovens and knits are the best choices because they gather easily. For this same reason, avoid heavy or firm, crisp fabrics. Try gathering a small piece of the fabric under consideration to determine if it's suitable.

Preparing the Fabric Strip

This is a simple process of cutting the strip to the desired length and width. I prefer an accent fabric for the piping, but you can use self fabric for a subtler effect.

1. Calculate the width of the fabric strip by doubling the desired finished width and adding 1¼ inches (for two seam allowances). If your seam allowances aren't the standard ⅝-inch wide, you need to add more or less to the width.

Width = (2 x desired width) + 1¼ inches.

2. Measure along the seamline to determine the length you need to cut your strip. Since you may lose some length when gathering the strip, add extra inches for insurance. You can always cut off the excess after the strip is applied to the garment edge.

3. Cut the fabric strip to the desired length and width. If you have substantial curves to navigate on the edge of your garment, you want to cut the strips on the bias or at least half bias. If the piping fabric has a bit of give on the crosswise grain, like in a knit, use the crosswise grain.

4. If you need to join several strips to achieve the desired length for the garment edge, join the strips with a diagonal seam. (See Step 2 of "Preparing the Binding" on page 77.) Place the ends of two strips together at a right angle. Pin a diagonal seam and open the lengths to ensure that you end up with a straight, joined strip. Refold and straight stitch as pinned. Trim the seam allowance to ¼ inch, press open, and trim any seam allowance extending past the edge of the joined strips.

Gathering the Strip

The gathering stitches go across the width of the fabric strip, so the amount of the gather determines the depth of the scallop. In other words, if you draw in lots of fabric to make the gathers, the scallop will be deeper than if the strip has minimal gathers. Experiment on a test strip before graduating to the garment (or accent) fabric. Increase the amount of gathering by making the stitch longer and/or increasing the upper tension. Decrease the amount of gathering by doing the opposite.

1. Before sewing, mark the location of each stitching line across the fabric width, using a fabric marker. The distance from one row of stitching to the next determines the length of the scallop. Place the first mark 1 inch from an end of the strip. (This distance allows easy manipulation of the fabric that's under the presser foot.)

2. Attach the gathering foot to the machine. Place the strip of fabric under the foot. Sew horizontally across the strip at the first marking. The fabric automatically gathers as you sew. Stop stitching at the opposite edge. Cut the threads, leaving a 1-inch long tail. This prevents the gathers from pulling out at any point during the construction process. Move to the opposite side to begin another row of stitching. Repeat this step at every mark along the length of the folded fabric until the entire strip is stitched.

Lyla's Notion　Water-Soluble Thread

I use water-soluble thread for Gathered Piping, Fray-Free & Easy Binding, and many other applications. It's valuable wherever you need temporary stitching to hold layers together or make placement lines.

Water-soluble thread is easy to use for machine-basting, plus you never have to pick out or brush off the stitches. Instead, dissolve the thread by merely spraying it with water when the instructions tell you to pull out the basting.

Start by machine winding water-soluble thread on the bobbin and threading it through the needle. Tension adjustments aren't necessary.

You only need to use the thread in either the needle or bobbin because, when one thread dissolves, the side of the stitching made with all-purpose sewing thread will come loose. But I prefer to place the thread in both the needle and the bobbin. Often, a technique requires that lines of stitching cover or cross the temporary stitching. With water-soluble thread in only one position, the permanent stitching won't release the all-purpose thread when the water-soluble thread is dissolved. You'll end up picking out the all-purpose thread.

With water-soluble thread, trims and bindings can be perfectly positioned inside and outside a garment. A line of stitching makes an ideal placement line because it's visible on both sides of the fabric and it dissolves in water. What a great way to save time and improve accuracy!

Storage is important. Keep the water-soluble thread in a plastic bag. This way, it won't degrade by absorbing moisture from the air. The plastic bag will also prevent an awful mistake: It reminds you that it isn't a regular sewing thread. At a trade show a woman told me she accidentally sewed a shirt with water-soluble thread. The first time she washed it, the garment fell apart! I was really impressed, because she sewed all of the pieces together again.

Creating the Piping

Simply fold the fabric strip to make the piping. To attach it to the garment, apply a placement line for guidance.

1. Fold the gathered strip in half lengthwise, with the wrong sides together. Baste the raw edges together using a ¼ inch seam allowance.

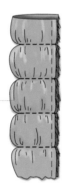

2. Pull out the fabric between each horizontal row of stitching. This gives the scallops definition.

3. Pin the piping to the right side of the garment with raw edges even, using a ⅝ inch seam allowance.

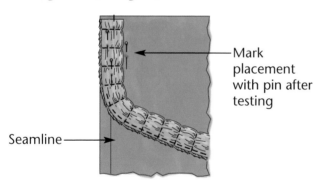

Mark placement with pin after testing

Seamline

4. Fold the seam allowance to the wrong side to assess the finished width of the scalloped piping. Remove the pins, shift the piping, and re-pin.

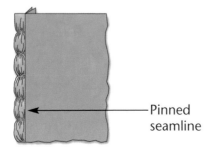

Pinned seamline

5. With the piping flat against the right side of the garment (as it will be sewn) place a pin on the garment fabric at the folded edge on the deepest part of the scallop.

6. Remove the piping. Measure the distance between the pin and the raw garment edge.

FAQ FREQUENTLY ASKED QUESTION

Why the placement line? Can't the edge of the piping be matched to the raw edge of the garment?

The placement line ensures that all of the scallops are the same size. Gathering has made the raw edges uneven, so the traditional piping placement method doesn't work.

7. With water-soluble thread in the needle and bobbin, baste the garment the desired distance from the raw edge. This line of stitching is the placement line for the piping.

8. Pin, then baste, the piping to the garment, positioning the outside (folded) edge of each scallop along the basted placement line.

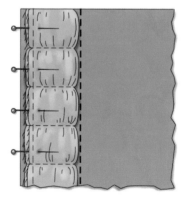

9. Apply the garment facing in the usual manner, and then understitch or edge stitch. Complete the garment.

A facing isn't the only option when you want a stable neckline that lasts the lifetime of a garment. Toss out the facing pattern and reach for fusible bias stay tape. This hidden edging, which ends up on the wrong side of the finished garment, controls curves without inhibiting the give you need for an attractive, flat neckline.

Facing-Free Neckline

Variation of Asymmetrical Tunic & Skirt

A curved neckline that doesn't have a facing often ends up with a stretched, twisted edge. There's a solution to this aggravating situation, and it's simpler than narrow hemming!

I use stay tape that's cut on the bias and has fusible on one side. The tape is stitched, and then fused, to the wrong side of the neckline. Since the final stitching is permanent, the garment edge is stabilized forever.

Until recently, all I did with fusible products was take them out of the package and fuse them in place. Then I realized that a combination of stitching and fusing opened a whole world of possibilities. Taking a new look at an old product sparked the development of other techniques in Ordinary to Extraordinary: Shaped Facing (see page 25), Curved Piecing (see page 38), and Jigsaw Appliqué (see page 21). It's amazing how a simple shift in perspective can make such a difference.

The tunic in the photo above is another example of how a small shift in a thought process can generate new possibilities. The garment neckline is asymmetrical for an unusual reason. The tunic is just two pattern pieces—but they aren't a back and front. Instead, I created left and right pattern pieces. This made it possible for me to design a different neckline shape for each side of the body. In addition, I no longer need to fuss with the edging at the tight inner corner. The tape just extends straight into the seam allowance.

Supplies

⅜-inch wide fusible bias stay tape

Mini Iron (optional)

Attaching the Tape

Sew or serge the fusible to the neck seam allowance.

1. Place the first few inches of the stay tape, fusible side up, on the wrong side of the garment. If the seam allowance is ⅝-inch wide, the tape and raw fabric edges aren't aligned. Instead, place the closest edge of the tape ¼ inch from the fabric edge. The goal is to position the entire tape on the seam allowance, with one edge butted against the seamline. If desired, you can baste or ink-mark along the seamline to establish a placement line.

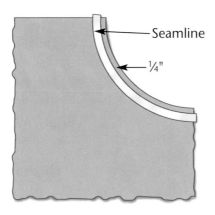

Seamline

¼"

2. Set the serger for a narrow 3-thread overlock stitch with a length that's a little longer than normal. This leaves more of the surface of the tape exposed for successful fusing (in a later step).

3. Start serging the tape to the neckline. Let the knives trim off any excess fabric beyond the edge of the tape.

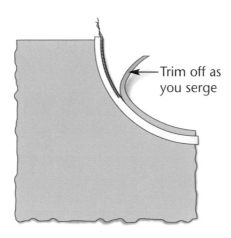

Trim off as you serge

FAQ **FREQUENTLY ASKED QUESTION**

Is it possible to apply this neckline treatment without using a serger?

You bet! Merely trim ¼ inch off the garment's neck edge before applying the tape. Now position the tape on the neckline with the edges even. Join them using an overcast or zigzag machine stitch.

4. Continue serging while easing the edge of the tape that lies along the raw edge of the fabric. (To ease, push it toward the stitching so that it won't stretch.) Keep the opposite side of the tape flat.

Fusing the Tape

It's easy to press the attached bias tape to the wrong side of the neckline because the tape stretches slightly.

1. Place the garment, wrong side up, on an ironing board. Using the seamline as a guide, fold the tape to the wrong side of the garment piece.

2. Using a Mini Iron or only the tip of an iron, join the fabric and tape by spot-fusing the shoulder seams, center front, and center back along the neckline with an up-and-down pressing motion. Ease the curve into shape with your fingers. Pins can be helpful, but remove them before pressing because they may mark the garment.

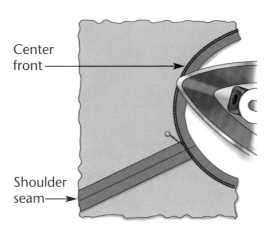

Center front

Shoulder seam

3. Spot-fuse the other points you have chosen and then fuse all points in between. Work on small sections so that it's easier to regulate the amount of stretch in the bias tape and get an even distribution of the fabric.

4. With the garment right side up, secure the tape with neckline stitching. Use a longer than normal straight stitch length, and a single or double needle. A double needle stitch prevents popped stitches because it stretches with the neckline curves.

FREQUENTLY ASKED QUESTION

Does this technique have other applications?

A turned edge with no facing or lining on a vest, blouse, or dress can also be eased with the tape. Simply follow the Facing-Free Neckline instructions. At the bust area stretch the bias stay tape as you fuse it along the seamline on the wrong side of the fabric pattern piece.

Lyla's Notion — Design Plus Fusible Stay Tape

Fusible bias stay tape is an essential item in my studio. Because it's both flexible and stable, it has many uses.

In fact, fusible bias tape simplifies and improves results in many aspects of garment construction. By adapting the Facing-Free Neckline instructions, you can control an armscye (armhole) by slightly stretching the tape as you sew it to the fabric edge, stabilize the shoulder seam of knit garments, and make a curved hem.

I prefer the ⅜-inch wide version of the tape that's fusible on one side. It's available in two weights, in black or white. The regular weight is a poly/cotton blend. The lighter weight is 100% polyester.

The Super Fine tape is good for light- to medium-light fabrics like silks, and rayons. It's effective for knits because the non-fusible side has a slick surface. The regular weight tape is the best choice for medium to heavy fabrics. If you're unsure which weight to use, go too light rather than too heavy.

The most common applications for straight-grain stay tape include placement along jacket roll lines, shoulder seams, and the tops of pockets or other long, straight edges. With the tape in place, the jacket collar will turn where the tape is positioned, shoulder seams won't stretch or distort, pockets won't droop, and long edges (like the front opening of a knee-length vest) will hang properly.

Every time you use this fusible tape you'll probably come up with even more ways to work with it. It's a simple product, yet it has numerous applications that will improve and speed up your sewing. I prefer the ⅜-inch wide version.

For locations that need stability, a straight-grain tape is the best choice. You forfeit the stretch of bias-cut stay tape, but gain stability. Since the straight grain tape is cut on the crosswise grain it can stretch slightly to help with the shaping and easing.

Best results are obtained with fusible stay tape if you apply it while using a combination of steam, heat, and pressure. Press the tape to the wrong side of the fabric with the fusible side down. Adjust your iron for steam, with the heat setting appropriate for the fabric. Always use a press cloth to protect delicate fabric. The fusing time may vary depending on the fabric type and the iron temperature. Always test the fusing procedure on a sample of the fabric.

Shelby

Zea Vest Collection

Bias Without Boundaries

Strips of fabric have long been used as binding on a garment, a quilt, or a home decor project. Yet there's an extraordinary array of applications for bias- and straight-cut fabric lengths. Make tubes, single- or double-fold tape. Then appliqué, stitch, twist, or weave them into enticing fabric or garment embellishments.

One of my favorite techniques in this chapter is Liana, which involves twisting and joining strips cut across the width of a piece of yardage. The look and feel of the fabric is totally changed! You end up with an interesting fabric for garment pieces or a unique binding or trim.

Bias strips of fabric sewn into tubes make fun Latticework yardage that drapes beautifully. It's an intriguing look that students often ask me to teach. They're delighted when they discover that the material is quickly completed because the work is done at the sewing machine, on a piece of water-soluble stabilizer.

Also in this chapter, you'll find ideas for using single-fold bias to frame appliqués, add design lines, and imitate the raised effect of trapunto quilting.

A mesh-like fabric offers the illusion of coverage without weight or bulk. The soft drape is suitable for an entire vest front, enticing inset, or eye-catching overlay. In any case, the starting point is bias-cut fabric tubes that are stitched to a water-soluble stabilizer.

Latticework Fabric

Zea Vest Collection

My inspiration comes from many sources— including designer garments. Several years ago, I saw a Carole Little vest that fascinated me. I'd never seen anything like the mesh effect created by the woven fabric tubes.

My concept of fashion fabric changed in an instant. Here was a simple mesh used the same way that I handled solid fabric. I was off to the studio to create my own Latticework.

To make a Latticework vest, cut a piece of stabilizer large enough for each vest front. Draw grid lines on the stabilizer to help you position the bias tubes. Now simply place the tubes in opposite directions, and stitch through all layers where the bias tubes intersect. The stabilizer stays attached until you've stitched the mesh to other garment pieces and bound the raw edges.

I discovered that the new fabric holds its shape quite nicely and it drapes well because I used bias-cut fabric for the tubes. This made it possible to fold out some slightly shaped areas of a pattern piece by simply folding the stabilizer paper in a dart fashion, and letting the Latticework mold over it.

Latticework edges that won't be sewn to another pattern piece are bound with bias binding. I like to continue the binding along the garment edges made from solid fabric pieces.

Supplies

½-inch bias tape maker, bias binder attachment foot for your sewing machine, Bias Buddy or Fasturn tube turner

#2 pencil (soft, moderately thick lead)

Quilter's ruler (see-through, plastic, with grid)

Water-soluble stabilizer paper

Suitable Fabric

Crinkled rayon, rayon challis, sand washed rayons and silks, and very soft cottons work well. Firmly woven fabrics are better than looser weaves. Some of the new textured rayons and lighter weight Tencels are also suitable.

Alluring peek-a-boo detailing is simple with a Latticework inset based on a 1-inch grid. Making an inset isn't difficult. Mark the inset area on the tissue pattern piece. Trace the design lines on to a piece of pattern tracing paper. Add seam allowances to the pattern piece wherever the inset is sewn to the garment. Don't add seam allowances where the edge of the inset is bound.

Lyla's Notion   Water–Soluble Paper Stabilizer

This product has several valuable applications, and a lot more will probably crop up as people continue to experiment with it. I've found it very helpful for transferring designs, doing heirloom sewing and machine embroidery, and making paper-pieced quilt templates.

It eliminates the shifting, sliding, and puckering that make some fabrics so annoying to work with. When all the sewing is complete, simply tear away as much of the stabilizer as possible, and then rinse the fabric in water. The paper dissolves almost instantly. (When you use a washaway stabilizer, always test your fabric to ensure it's washable.) It doesn't make the fabric stiff or leave a residue.

I experimented with a variety of stabilizers when creating the Latticework technique. Hot Stuff worked well. It's extremely crisp and had enough substance to keep the grainline and, consequently the grid, from shifting. Hot Stuff had to be ironed off or put in a 350° oven. The fabric had to be heat resistant to that temperature, and it was nerve–racking watching my garments cook. I glued my feet to the floor, forcing myself to watch it every second.

My favorite water-soluble stabilizer is Design Plus. Although a paper product, it's transparent enough for tracing pattern pieces, grid lines, and designs. It doesn't shift as you work, holds its shape, and is strong enough to withstand handling.

Hot Stuff is intended for costuming, and it became very hard to buy. So I went in search of a replacement. I tried other heat-soluble stabilizers, but they were too soft, which caused the grid to shift off-grain.

Tear-away stabilizers aren't a good choice for Latticework. They're acceptable where the strips are sewn together at intersections, but they're difficult to remove after the binding is applied.

Adapting a Pattern

I like to use a garment pattern that's designed for bound edges because there's no need to adjust it for the Latticework Fabric. However, you can adapt almost any pattern if you remember some basic guidelines.

1. The edges of Latticework fabric must be finished with bias binding if they aren't seamed. Before making your mesh-like fabric, remove the seam allowances from the pattern piece edges that will be bound on the finished garment.

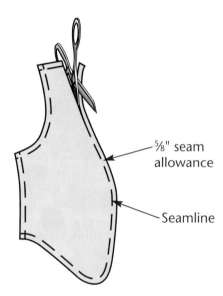

⅝" seam allowance

Seamline

2. Anywhere the Latticework garment piece joins another pattern piece you need a seam allowance.

3. Analyze your pattern before you decide where to place the Latticework. Avoid joining two Latticework pieces with a seam because the seam allowances show. Sandwiching the Latticework seam allowances between an adjacent fabric garment piece and its corresponding lining or facing is a great way to hide the raw edges.

4. I won't make a piece of Latticework for anything larger than a vest front. The yardage sags when it's too large, and it may catch on things when the finished garment is worn.

Preparing the Stabilizer Shapes

A piece of stabilizer is the base for your Latticework. This stabilizer is slightly larger than the pattern piece shape.

1. Use a pencil to trace the pattern piece cutting lines on to your stabilizer.

2. Cut out the shape with a border that extends 1 inch beyond the pattern cutting lines. Make the border the same width around the entire pattern piece. You need a stabilizer shape for each garment piece. In other words, if your tissue pattern piece says "Cut 2," then you need two stabilizer shapes.

3. Draw horizontal and vertical lines on one pattern piece to create a grid. A 1- to 1½-inch grid works well for a vest front or an inset. Remember that curved parts of the body may protrude from the grids if the holes are too large. In this situation, the Latticework Fabric catches and clings, rather than drapes along the body.

FAQ FREQUENTLY ASKED QUESTION

Does it matter where the grid lines are positioned?

I make the first horizontal line at the widest part of the pattern piece, close to the center. I usually measure to make sure I don't end up with a tube right next to a seam. The vertical lines are best placed in a manner that results in as many tubes as possible ending up at the shoulders. For an inset, it's important to center the vertical lines on the pattern piece so both sides are symmetrical. The inset's bound edge is a good place to start measuring the placement of all of the lines for the horizontal tubes.

FREQUENTLY ASKED QUESTION

Is it important that the grid is perfect?

Not "perfect" . . . that word isn't in my dictionary! But the grid should be carefully drawn so the lines stay parallel to one another. A small variation doesn't show on a finished piece, but a large one does. If I don't have a grid to trace, like the one in the Zea Vest pattern, I use a clear, plastic ruler, preferably long enough to run one continuous mark across the pattern piece.

4. Latticework needs to be symmetrical if it's used in the same location on the right and left side of a garment. That means the grids on each stabilizer shape must match. Place the gridded stabilizer shape under the other shape that you cut out. Now trace the lines on the remaining shape.

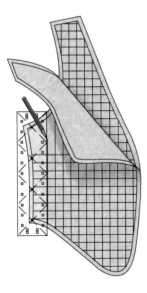

5. The grid on one of the shapes is on the wrong side of the stabilizer. You may want to transfer the marks to the front of the paper for better visibility when you're working at your machine. It's a good idea to label the right side of the stabilizer, to make sure that you don't end up with two left fronts or two right fronts.

Making Bias Tubes

Since the tubes are fairly short, it isn't necessary to cut the fabric strips from continuous bias. The width of the strips varies the look of the Latticework Fabric. For the ¼-inch wide tubes for my vests, I cut generous 1-inch-wide strips.

1. I use a rotary cutter and ruler, and then cut the strips diagonally across the entire width of the fabric yardage.

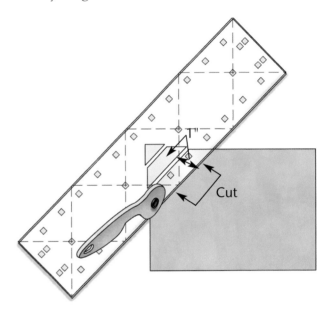

2. Testing is important. Every fabric reacts differently, so your tubes may not turn out as you envisioned. Cut a single strip of bias fabric to the desired width and make a tube. If the width is to your liking, cut out all the strips that you need.

FREQUENTLY ASKED QUESTION

Are the fabric tubes pressed at this point?

It isn't necessary. There's no reason to press the finished tubes unless they're wrinkled. In this case, give the Latticework a good steaming, without a lot of pressure. Heavy pressing may flatten some fabrics.

3. There are several ways to make the fabric tubes for the Latticework fabric. After exploring many options, I've discovered that certain notions make the job easier and faster. Take a look at the tube-making supplies featured at the bottom of this page.

Choosing a Stitch

The Latticework fabric stays together because the bias tubes are joined at every intersection.

This is where you can have some fun with the stitches on your machine. Use straight or decorative machine stitches or motifs, or even hand stitch the tubes for an invisible effect.

An electronic machine with an auto–stop control makes it simple to do a single decorative stitch. If you don't have this feature, sew a straight stitch diagonally across the intersection.

Always practice your stitch choice on a sample before you start working on the real thing.

Lyla's Notion   Bias Tape Maker, Bias Buddy, Binding Foot, and Fasturn Tube Turner

A bias tape maker or a Bias Buddy help you fold and press a strip in half lengthwise. To form a tube, machine-sew the folded edges together.

With a Fasturn Tube Turner, simply sew together the lengthwise edges of a bias fabric strip (right sides facing), and then turn it right side out with the correct size tube.

My favorite tools are a sewing machine binding attachment and binder foot. In one step, one of these notions can double-fold a flat strip of bias fabric and sew it together. Be sure to check the manufacturer's instructions. Some feet fold the fabric twice, others need pre-folded bias. If you have to fold the bias first, the foot isn't a time-saver.

You can also use a binding attachment to apply binding to the edges of the Latticework Fabric by inserting the edge of your mesh fabric into the opening between the two layers of the bias strip as you sew.

Fasturn Tube Turner courtesy of Crowing Touch

Presser foot courtesy of Husqvarna Viking Sewing Machines

I like designing with fabric tubes, so I constantly experiment with notions that give me attractive, painless results. My favorites are the Bias Buddy and Fasturn Tube Turner at left, bias tape maker in the center, and binding foot to the right.

Assembling the Grid

It's best to work with all of the bias tubes beside you, at your sewing machine.

1. Start at the longest vertical grid line on the right side of a stabilizer shape. Place a bias tube along this line. You want to start here to ensure that you have enough long tubes. It's difficult to center a bias tube on a line, so place one long edge along the marked line. Extend both ends of the tube at least ½ inch past the stitching line for the finished garment shape. The stitching line is the seamline on edges with seams, and the actual edge of the shape on pieces that are finished with binding. If you're making matching pieces for the left and right side of a garment, they need to be symmetrical. I place bias tubes to the left of the grid line on one stabilizer shape, and to the right on the other. Align the top of every horizontal bias tube with a grid line.

2. Place a second, horizontal, bias tube across the first. Position the second tube so that it's across the widest part of the stabilizer shape and the upper edge is aligned with the grid line.

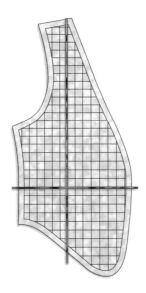

3. Use your chosen stitch to sew through the intersection of the bias tubes and the stabilizer under-

neath. Pinning the tubes to the stabilizer makes this step very awkward. There's no reason to keep the tubes in position, except at the point where the two tubes cross one another. That's one of the things that makes this technique so fast and easy.

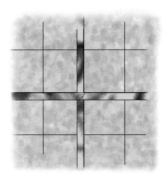

4. Add only one bias tube at a time from now on. It doesn't matter whether you add vertical or horizontal tubes, as long as you work out from the first position. You could do all the horizontal, and then all the vertical strips. Make sure that you weave the crosswise and lengthwise bias tubes. This gives your fabric a more pleasing texture than having all the crosswise tubes on the top and all the lengthwise tubes on the bottom.

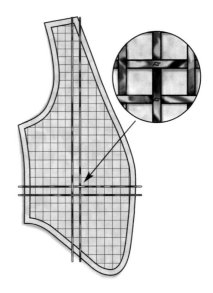

5. As you add each tube, stitch through the layers at every intersection, then move on to the next strip. Continue adding more bias tubes in this fashion until your Latticework is complete.

6. Straight stitch just inside the pattern cutting lines on the stabilizer shape. This holds the bias tubes in place at the edges after the 1-inch border is cut away.

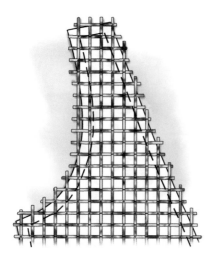

Assembling a Garment

Construct the garment as usual. You don't want seam allowances or tube ends to show through the woven bias tubes.

1. Place the right side of the Latticework shape against the right side of the adjacent garment piece with the raw edges even. Now place the right side of the facing or lining on the wrong side of the Latticework.

2. Stitch the pieces together. Trim the excess Lattice-work seam allowance width to ¼- to ⅜-inch.

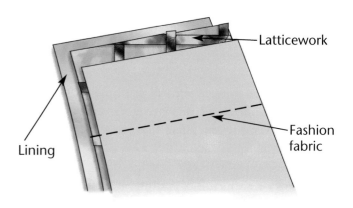

Latticework

Lining

Fashion fabric

3. Press the garment piece and facing or lining away from the Latticework.

Binding the Edges

Any Latticework edges that aren't sewn to another pattern piece need to be covered with bias binding. I continue the binding along other, non-mesh, edges on the garment.

My fusible thread binding technique, on page 41, is a superb way to bind the edges while the paper stabilizer is still attached. Edge stitch the binding to the Latticework rather than stitching in the ditch. This is

---

inspiration point

before assembling the garment, you can add decorative tubes to the grid. Simply swirl a completed bias tube on the Latticework as desired, and edge stitch it in place. Although you only need to tack the decorative bias tube at the intersections, stitching one edge along the entire length is faster.

the only way to permanently hold together the two layers of binding. A binding attachment works well for this process.

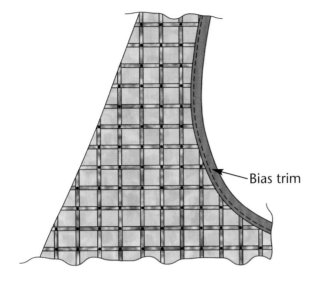

Bias trim

Removing the Stabilizer

This is the end of the process, and one that's a lot of fun to do.

1. Tear away as much of the water-soluble paper as possible.

2. Place the garment in a sink of water to remove the remaining paper. Warm water dissolves the paper faster. If necessary, gently agitate the garment.

3. If too much paper pulp accumulates, drain the sink and add fresh water.

4. You can wash the Latticework in a machine set for a gentle cycle. Put the work in a lingerie bag before placing it in the machine. This prevents the Lattice-work from catching on things in the machine.

inspiration point

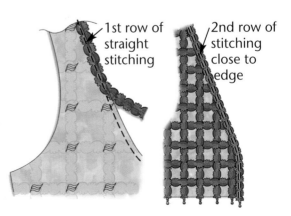

Zea Vest Collection

Pushing the concept of fabric even further, why not turn a favorite trim into Latticework? My unique version is constructed almost the same way as the original.

First, preshrink the trim.

Follow the instructions for adapting a pattern, preparing the stabilizer shapes, choosing a stitch, and assembling the grid. In Step 6 of "Assembling the Grid," trim off the border ¼ inch outside the cutting lines.

Rather than binding, use trim to edge the garment. Place the wrong side of the trim-binding on the wrong side of the garment edge. Edge stitch close to the inner edge of the trim-binding.

Fold the trim–binding to the right side of the garment and edge-stitch the loose edge to the garment. Don't apply trim-binding to the hem. Instead, add some beads to the bottom of each piece of trim.

1st row of straight stitching

2nd row of stitching close to edge

Stunning detail doesn't have to be difficult to create. Walk away from endless hours at the ironing board because you don't have to turn under raw appliqué edges nor pin it to the garment. There are great adhesive products on the market that make the entire process very easy. Just press a shape on your garment and cover the raw edges with single fold bias tape.

Instant Appliqué

Zea Vest Collection

H ere's a pin-less, painless procedure for attaching an abstract shape to a garment, then framing the piece with strips of bias that cover the raw edges.

Developing this unique appliqué is simple. A piece of fabric is your starting point. Choose a small fabric treasure, woven fabric strips, an embroidered motif . . . even a sample of your favorite stitching or a picture transferred to fabric.

What a superb opportunity this gives you. You can showcase a piece of embellished or texturized fabric that you made when trying out one of the other techniques in this book. For example, use a Stitch Sampler swatch that's shaped like a triangle with curved edges. Another option is creating a small work using the Gathered Texture technique, and then cutting it into an interesting shape. Latticework and Rhapsody Fabric also work well as Instant Appliqués. So you create a small piece of fabric using one of those techniques, and then apply it as your appliqué.

A bias tape maker can turn almost any fabric into strips that you can use as a frame. Then you can use a straight, blind hem, or decorative stitch to secure the lengths to the garment.

Supplies

Appliqué fabric

Clover Bias Tape Maker

Contrasting fabric for bias

Edge stitch or zipper presser foot

Paper larger than the appliqué

Pattern tracing paper larger than the appliqué

Pencil

Press cloth (optional)

Temporary adhesive spray

Ultra Soft Double Sided Fusible (optional)

Suitable Fabric

As far as the strips go, a light- to medium-weight fabric like rayon challis, soft cotton, or Tencel work well. These fabrics are just suggestions; I don't want to discourage you from experimenting with other types of materials.

Bias strips frame an abstract fabric shape. Prints are ideal because you don't have to use fancy stitching. Merely straight stitch the bias to the garment. In one step you cover the raw fabric edges of the appliqué and add interest. Extend the bias strips beyond the fabric shape to make the effect even more dramatic.

Designing an Appliqué

You needn't be an artist to develop a one-of-a-kind appliqué. Have some fun and think simple.

My appliqués are based on shapes that I find in books and magazines. I look for simple forms, and then tweak the outer lines a little here and there. This is much easier than drawing something from scratch.

Abstract and large shapes work well, but simple geometric forms can be interesting. Whatever you choose, pay attention to the outer edges. Avoid inner corners so that you don't have to miter a bias strip. Look for softly curved shapes. This way, the bias strip can simply bend a bit to cover the edges of the appliqué.

The size of the appliqué is proportional to the garment and the finished width of the bias strips. For example, a ½-inch wide strip looks best with a design that's at least 3 x 4 inches. For a smaller appliqué, try a ¼-inch wide bias strip. It's best to keep the appliqué no larger than 5 x 6 inches. These are just guidelines.

Planning the Placement

Positioning a design over a seam is a great way to create an expensive designer look because the image is planned with the entire garment in mind, rather than plopped on one section.

Use the pattern sketch to identify positions that enhance the appliqué and garment. Now identify seams that the appliqué could cover. A shoulder seam is ideal on a vest. Don't run the design over a seam that makes the garment look like a tube, such as a side seam on the body.

Your appliqué can be positioned almost anywhere on a garment. The key is to plan its placement so that you're working flat when attaching the bias strips. Since the shoulder seam is made before the side seam on a vest, it's easy to join the shoulder, lay the vest flat on a table, pin the design up and over the shoulder, attach it, and then complete the garment.

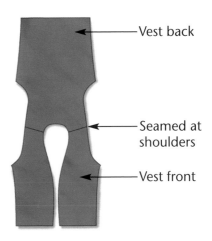

Vest back

Seamed at shoulders

Vest front

Making an Appliqué Pattern

In a few simple steps you can create a paper "frame" that helps you determine a pleasing position for the appliqué.

1. If you plan to use customized work for the appliqué, create the piece now. You can make the treatment on a fabric square that's larger than the appliqué pattern, then cut out the shape later.

2. Cut the garment pieces from the fashion fabric and assemble them to the point where you have completed the seam over which the appliqué will be placed.

3. Trace the appliqué shape in the center of a square piece of paper.

4. Draw cutting lines ¼ inch beyond the traced appliqué shape on the paper. Cut out the shape.

5. Place the paper frame on the appliqué fabric. Shift the paper until you're happy with the appearance of the fabric inside the frame. This is important when your fabric has a print that needs an attractive location on the appliqué shape. Since bias strips are sewn around the edges of the appliqué, the finished appliqué can be as much as ½ inch wider than the paper frame.

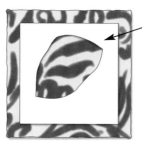
Interesting design inside fabric frame

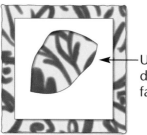
Unappealing design inside fabric frame

6. Place the frame on top of a piece of pattern tracing paper. Trace the appliqué shape on to the bottom layer by running a pencil around the inside of the frame. Remove the frame. Cut the appliqué pattern from the tracing paper.

Sizing the Bias

Choose a finished width that complements the size and shape of the appliqué. The bias fabric strip that you use to hide the raw edges of the applique can be any size that you desire. It's best to experiment with several widths so that you know which one is perfect for the print, fabric weight, and overall appearance of the garment.

1. Decide the width of the bias strips for the appliqué frame on the finished garment. Single fold bias with a ½ inch finished width works well for most appliqués. In this case, start with 1-inch wide bias strips.

FAQ FREQUENTLY ASKED QUESTION

Is there an easy way to make narrower bias strips?

There are two options. You can use double folded bias as shown on the Freedom Wrap by the Function Meets Fashion introduction on page 1. Bias tubes, which are explained in Latticework Fabric on page 97, also work well. If narrower strips are used, trim 1/16 inch from the appliqué perimeter.

2. Cut enough bias strips from contrasting fabric to make about 2 yards of single fold bias. This is enough for most designs. The bias doesn't have to be continuous because the strips only need to be long enough to cover a side of the appliqué and extend past it to create design lines.

3. Turn each strip into single fold bias using a Clover bias tape maker.

Applying the Appliqué

You won't believe how quickly this process goes. It's important to complete your project within a few days because the temporary adhesive will lose its strength and the appliqué will pull away from the garment.

1. Place the wrong side of the appliqué pattern on the right side of the contrasting or texturized fabric and cut out the shape.

2. Spray the entire wrong side of the appliqué with temporary adhesive.

3. With both pieces right side up, rub the appliqué on to the garment.

FAQ FREQUENTLY ASKED QUESTION

Can the bias be sprayed with temporary adhesive and then pressed on to the appliqué and garment?

I prefer pins because the adhesive makes it harder to place the bias. This interferes with the simplicity of creating the design without a lot of planning. Ultra Soft Double Sided Fusible is a better alternative. Place it on the wrong side of the strip, peel off the paper backing, and pin it on the garment. When you're happy with the position of all the strips, press them. This fusing holds everything in place and helps stabilize the decorative stitch.

Applying the Bias

Cover the raw edges of the appliqué and create an overall design with strips of bias. Strategically placing some strips over seamlines will give your garment a boutique look. Think through the construction process so that you can work flat.

1. Plan the position of the first piece of bias on the appliqué. Choose one that allows the start of the bias (a raw edge) to be hidden in a seam allowance. Pin the bias, right side up, on the appliqué so that it covers ¼ inch of the appliqué's raw edge.

2. If you have several appliqué shapes, visually link them by running the bias strips from one shape to the next. Think of this as building a giant puzzle that has more than one solution.

3. Continue pinning bias to the appliqué edges. Make sure that the raw bias ends are in seam allowances or hidden under an overlapping piece of bias. Secure the bias with just enough pins to hold it in place. Continue until all appliqué edges are covered with bias strips.

4. Set your machine for a straight stitch. Use an edge, blind hem, or zipper presser foot to improve accuracy. Position the work on the sewing machine bed, right side up. Take the first stitch manually, turning the fly wheel to make sure that the needle clears the foot and is in the desired location. Edge stitch the bias strip to the garment along one side, and then stitch the other long side of the bias in the same manner. If the thread is a good match, the stitching is barely visible.

FAQ FREQUENTLY ASKED QUESTION

How do you work a bias strip around a curved edge?

This is a simple process because the bias is so flexible. Simply bend it to the desired shape as you position it around the appliqué. Slightly ease the inside edge of the bias while gently stretching the outer edge.

inspiration point

attaching the bias with decorative machine stitches also looks great. I particularly like the ones that are flat on one side and can run along the edge of the bias strip. (In other words, regardless where the needle swings to the left, it always returns to the far right to stitch on that side.) Keep in mind that decorative stitches take longer, but the results are well worth the extra effort!

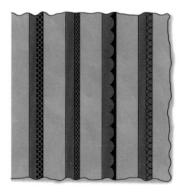

A lush fabric enhances the yoke and center front panel on this jacket. Surprisingly, the rich texture of the green tweed wasn't created on a loom. Instead, fabric strips were twisted and then seamed together at a sewing machine. Then the garment shapes were cut from the Liana fabric and assembled with the rest of the garment pieces, which are Tencel fabric.

Liana Stitching

Shelby

Liana is a French name that means to twine around. That's exactly what this technique involves: strips of fabric are twisted and sewn together to create a dense, textural surface. The effect is ideal wherever you want contrasting fabric on a garment, but prefer an understated look. Other garments call for a high-impact treatment, so Liana Stitching is perfect as a bold edging.

The technique was inspired by a bathroom renovation. A fabric-covered shelf had to go, because it didn't fit the new color scheme. I never paid much attention to the piece: I just bought it, hung it up, and used it. But when I took it down I convinced myself that if I took it apart I could cover it with another fabric and continue using it in the new color scheme. I discovered that the strips of fabric were merely twisted, and then wrapped side-by-side on a metal frame. As I updated the shelf, I wondered what would happen if I stitched the fabric lengths together rather than wrapping them on a frame.

Liana was born.

The technique is most suitable for any garment part designed for medium-weight fabric. A continuous strip of fabric must be used for the Liana technique. At first, I sewed together the ends of fabric lengths. Then a woman who makes rag rugs taught me an easier method.

Supplies

Empty plastic box for sewing machine needles

Matching or decorative thread with a soft hand*

Quilter's clear, gridded ruler

Rotary cutter and self-healing mat (optional)

Transparent tape

*See "Choosing Thread" on page 109.

Suitable Fabric

Fabric with a soft hand is most effective. Consider knit yardage, old sweaters, Polar Fleece, Berber, or sweatshirt material, textured knits, wovens, or a bouclé. The raw edges are exposed, so expect wovens to ravel. A fabric that's different on each side can add more dimension to the work, since both are visible when it's finished. The strips can be twisted to the inside so that one side is never visible. In general, a moderately thick fabric is more interesting, but is certainly not a limit.

Before

After

No need to endlessly search for a complementary fabric to enhance a garment. Use what you have to make something entirely new. First cut the yardage into strips, and then twist and rejoin the new strips. The process is simple because you twist the strips as they're attached. Many variables affect the finished appearance, so it's best to test your plans. This is the best way to ensure that you achieve the desired appearance and fabric weight before cutting the entire yardage into strips.

Determining Strip Width

The width of the fabric strips greatly changes the finished effect. It's best to try several test swatches. The goal is to create fabric that has a suitable weight and drape for the desired garment. The thicker or bulkier the fabric, the narrower the strips need to be.

1. Launder the fabric. Cut ⅜-, ¾-, and 1-inch wide fabric strips, along the fabric's crossgrain. Use one strip to make each sample. A stable non-woven fabric like Polar Fleece works well when the strips are ¼- to ⅜-inch wide. A woven fabric that ravels isn't a good candidate for ¼-inch wide strips. Wider strips are possible in thin, non-bulky fabrics.

2. Working with one width at a time, join two strips according to the directions that follow. Make several short rows with strips of the same width, so that you have a good representation of the finished effect. I like making a 4-inch wide, 6-inch long piece to evaluate the look, feel, weight, and drape. You might want to launder the finished piece before assessing the results.

Estimating Yardage

You won't lose a lot of length in the strip as it's twisted. But this isn't a guarantee because the thickness and width of the strips affect the results. Do a test swatch!

Liana Stitching has so many variables that it's difficult to offer a formula for calculating the additional yardage needed for garment pieces. Allowing 25 to 30% more than the pattern specifies should be plenty.

Preparing the Fabric Strips

You need a continuous length of fabric.

1. Spread the yardage, one layer thick, on a fabric cutting table.

2. Place a quilter's ruler along a crosswise edge, from selvage to selvage. Measure the desired strip width from the raw fabric edge. Using a rotary cutter and self-healing mat (or scissors), cut through one selvage and continue across the width of the yardage. Stop ⅜ inch from the selvage edge on the opposite side.

3. Move the ruler so that it's the desired width from the newest cut at the crosswise edge. Starting at the selvage edge that you didn't cut through, cut across the width of the yardage. Again stop ⅜ inch from the opposite selvage edge. Continue cutting strips from alternate sides of the yardage.

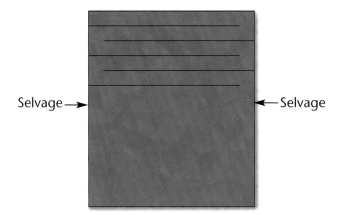

Selvage →   ← Selvage

Choosing Thread

You can use a regular sewing thread in a matching color, or choose a decorative product.

Use the same or complementary threads in the needle and bobbin. Since the fabric is flipped as it's stitched, both the needle and bobbin stitching are visible on the fabric.

The top thread shows on one row, the bobbin on the next. A regular thread is less conspicuous because it blends with the fabric. To add dimension, choose a decorative product. Whatever thread you select, keep in mind that it affects the stiffness of the finished fabric. I wouldn't use a stiff or coarse metallic thread. But the soft hand of a rayon or Halo Thread is ideal.

Lyla's Notion   Homemade Fabric Guide

Once you cut the fabric lengths and choose a stitch to hold the strips together, it's time to create a high-tech, ultra-fancy guide. Actually, this little gadget is as simple as it gets, and you don't have to buy a thing because the supplies are probably close at hand.

When attached, this homemade fabric guide notion helps you guide the fabric strips. You need this because Liana depends on careful placement of the left and right fabric strips under the sewing machine presser foot so that the needle stitching is centered over the inner edges of the two strips.

Stand the needle box on its side, aligned with the front of the presser foot. Ensure that it's centered on the needle. Secure the box with transparent tape: start the tape on the machine bed, wrap it up and over the plastic needle box, and on to the machine bed on the other side of the needle box.

There's nothing fancy about this handy tool. A needle box taped to the front of your machine guides and separates the Liana fabric (left) from the new strip that's being attached on the right.

Starting the New Fabric

You still need to choose an appropriate stitch, but it's best to set yourself up at the machine before experimenting.

1. Wrap a short length of transparent tape over the front of the toes on the presser foot. This prevents the fabric strips from catching on the foot during stitching.

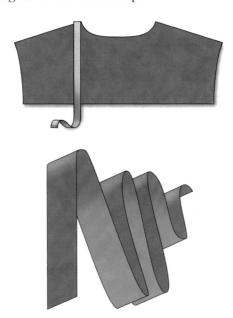

Fold tape from top to bottom

2. Measure the length of the pattern piece at its longest point and add a few extra inches. Measure this length from the beginning of a continuous strip of fabric. Fold back the strip at this point. You now have two lengths of full-width strips.

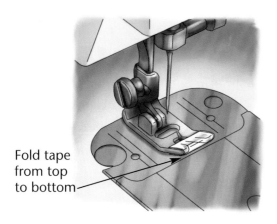

3. Put the folded end of the strip under the presser foot with the shorter length to the left. Drop the needle into the strip at the fold. The short end of the strip goes to the left of the homemade guide. Place the other side of the folded strip to the right, with the excess in your lap. Lower the presser foot.

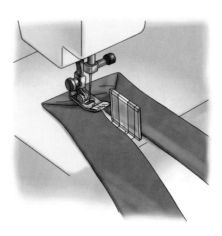

Choosing a Stitch

This is another opportunity to play with the stitches on your machine. A decorative stitch 4 mm or wider is suitable for Liana. Lengthen a dense stitch.

A simple "sewn-out" zigzag (several stitches on the left swing and several more to the right while advancing to the next spot) does a nice job of joining the strips. Set the width to at least 4 mm or as wide as your machine permits. Start with a 2 mm stitch length and then adjust it as desired.

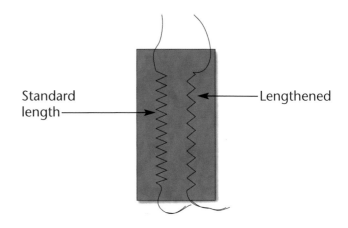

Standard length   Lengthened

Doing the Twist

Now you're ready to twist and sew the strips together. The first couple of rows won't look good. The finished effect starts to emerge after several strips are joined together.

1. With the short side of the strip to the left and the longer side to the right of the needle case guide, and with the presser foot down, you're ready to stitch. Lightly twist the first 6 to 8 inches of the strip on the right. The amount of twist isn't as important as maintaining consistency.

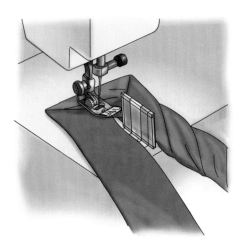

2. Start stitching the twisted strip on the right to the flat strip on the left. Make sure that the stitch is centered over the inner edges of the strips. Continue twisting and sewing until you reach the end of the strip on the left. Stop with the needle up and lift the presser foot. Don't break the threads.

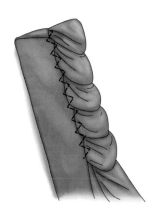

FAQ FREQUENTLY ASKED QUESTION

Is it possible to twist both strips from the very start?

Yes, but it's a bit more difficult. It is, however, the best route to take when you're working with a bulky fabric. Twisting both strips gives you an even height to the left and right of the needle for the first row.

3. Pull the first row of stitching away from the machine without breaking the threads. Flip the stitched strip over so that the fold is now closest to you. Place it to the left of the needle case guide, under the presser foot.

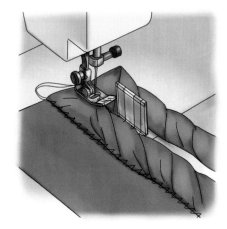

4. Fold the unstitched length of the continuous strip and place it to the right of the needle and handmade guide. The strip goes under the presser foot, with the excess length resting in your lap.

5. Drop the presser foot. Twist and stitch the right strip to the Liana fabric on the left. At this point, it's time to start adding additional rows of twisted fabric. You're still working with the same fabric strip, merely flipping it over every time that you reach the end of a row. (See Steps 2 and 3 on this page.) Continue building your Liana yardage in this manner until you have a width suitable for (slightly larger than) the pattern piece.

Assembling the Garment

Once the Liana fabric is completed, simply cut out the pattern piece in the usual manner and then construct the garment.

Don't worry about stitches unraveling between the twisted strips. Decorative stitches are quite stable on the thick Liana fabric. Handle the seam allowances as you would any woven fabric. In fact, you can even overlock them.

---

inspiration point

Liana is a superb trim for garment edges. The fold-over braid at the front opening of this vest started as narrow (⅜-inch wide) strips of Polar Fleece. Because the strips were narrower, it was easier to achieve an even look on the first row. I twisted the strips on both sides of the needle when starting to stitch. This vest has six joined fabric lengths. I simply folded the Liana binding over the garment edge so that three strips are on the outside, and three are on the inside. To use the same idea for decorative trim (not shown), just twist together as many strips as desired, and topstitch in position on the garment.

LaConner

The quilterly trapunto effect may look like a traditional piece of stitching, but that's not the case. This imitative technique takes advantage of a fabric's loft, nap, or texture to create volume and camouflages the stitching that makes the effect possible.

Faux Trapunto

Quilters spend many hours mastering the skills needed to build intricate trapunto effects. You can achieve a similar effect on your sewing machine in less than half the time using a plush, napped, or textured fabric.

Traditionally, trapunto and its variations (cording, Italian trapunto, padded appliqué, or stuffed work) involve layering fabrics, stitching a design, and then stuffing it to achieve a raised effect. The finished work looks gorgeous, but the creation process is so tedious!

I stumbled onto faux trapunto while preparing for a class on working with bias. I decided to topstitch curved strips to the surface of a jacket. The bias strips were the same fabric as the jacket: a textured cotton from the home decor department of a fabric store.

Turning the strips into tubes and stitching them in position, I discovered that the center of each piece puffed out. The four layers of the tube (top, bottom, and two seam allowances) filled in each tube. When I started wearing the jacket, students kept asking if it was trapunto.

In the following instructions you'll also learn how to create a single–fold strip for Polar Fleece. The crosswise grain of Polar Fleece has a lot of give, so it isn't necessary to use bias-cuts strips.

Supplies

Edge stitch or zipper presser foot (optional)

Fasturn Tube Turner (optional)

Matching or invisible thread

Stiletto

Transparent zigzag or an open-toe embroidery presser foot (Method 3)

Ultra Soft Double Sided Fusible (optional, for Polar Fleece)

Water-Soluble Thread (optional)

Creating a Design

A Faux Trapunto design can have curved or straight lines, randomly placed on a garment. In later steps, these lines become raised surfaces made from single- or double-fold "tape," or tubes of bias fabric, or crosswise strips of fleece or knit material.

It's best to keep the design lines separate, so they don't overlap. You can develop more elaborate motifs, perhaps creating a design of straight and gently curved bias. I start by placing raw fabric strips on the right side of the garment. Then I just move the pieces around until I'm happy with the appearance. Sometimes, I merely sketch the lines on a piece of paper.

A pinwheel is possible with short curved strips coming from a common starting point on the garment. Or consider staggering the beginning of several strips across a surface.

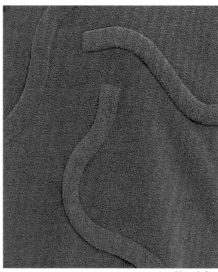
Kanisha

Polar Fleece is a perfect example of suitable fabric for Faux Trapunto. It has loft so, like other fabrics with texture or a plush surface, the multiple fabric layers create the effect. Other suitable materials include home decor cotton with a woven texture, boiled wool, sweater knits, velour, and acrylics. The visual interest of the finished garment is improved by placing some of the trapunto elements over a seam. You won't see this design element on low-end garments.

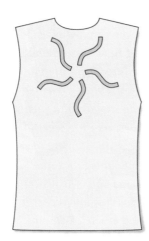

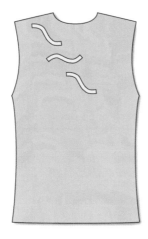

Making Fabric Strips

The fabric strips are the secret of the Faux Trapunto technique. Each one is placed on a design line and topstitched to the base fabric. There's no need to stuff the design area.

1. Cut bias strips from the fabric. Make the strips long enough for each of the design lines. Cut the strips wide enough to make double-fold bias. You can cut strips on the crosswise grain if your fabric has a lot of crosswise give. A finished width of ⅜ to ¾ inch is nice, although this depends on your design.

2. Fold and press each strip into double-fold tape. Straight-stitch the long folded edges together. This stitching might be visible on the finished work. If you suspect this will happen, sew the folded edges to-

gether with Water-Soluble Thread or use bias tubes, as explained on page 97. You might also consider bias tubes if the fabric is suitable for turning with a Fas-turn Tube Turner. Instructions are on page 98.

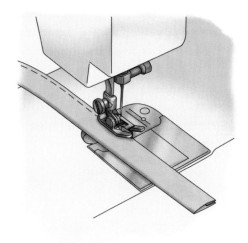

FREQUENTLY ASKED QUESTION

What do you do when a fabric, Polar Fleece for example, is too thick to make double-fold tape?

Try making your own single fold tape since the fabric is too heavy to feed through a bias tape maker. Fuse a strip of Ultra Soft Double Sided Fusible down the center of the wrong side of the strip. Remove the paper backing. Fold both long edges to the middle of the wrong side, steam, and finger-press in place. Don't flatten the fabric by pressing it with the iron. Once this is done, you have a single fold tape to place on the garment with the raw edges toward the garment fabric.

Lyla's Notion   Stiletto

I couldn't live without a stiletto. It's an integral tool in my studio because it's so versatile. Among its many uses, a stiletto helps me hold fabric or trim exactly where I want it during stitching. While sliding work under the presser foot, I can use a stiletto to maintain pressure on the fabric and then lower the presser foot. The stiletto can remain in position until the work is almost under the needle. You can use it to feed plush fabric under the presser foot and control slippery or sticky fabric. It's a great help when my fingers can't reach.

I highly recommend the stiletto for the Faux Trapunto technique because the raw fabric ends of the bias need to be turned under. In most cases, you're trying to pin eight layers of fabric to the garment background. The first time I did this, I bent a straight pin and stabbed myself. Then I bled on my cream colored fabric. "There has to be a better way to do this," I decided. The stiletto was the solution.

A stiletto helps you control pieces of fabric and trim while they're under, or near, the presser foot. This is a great tool because it can be used wherever your fingers can't go. The quill stiletto, at left, is terrific for fine fabrics and won't break your needle if you sew on it. The Clover stiletto, on the right, is strong and has a handle that's easy to hold.

Placing the Strips

It's easiest to work with the garment while the pieces are still flat, but you can add Faux Trapunto to a finished garment.

1. Assemble the garment pieces until you have completed the seam over which the strips will be positioned. If you want to place the design over a shoulder seam, for example, sew the shoulder seam, finish the raw seam allowances, and press them open. Now you're ready to position the design strips.

2. Pin all of the strips on the garment in the desired positions. Strips travel easily around curves because they're either bias-cut or made of stretchy fabric.

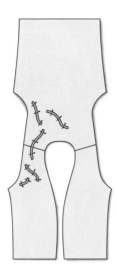

3. Hang the garment on a wall. Step back several feet and assess the appearance. Adjust the design until pleased with the look.

Sewing the Strips

There are three choices for this part of the technique. Choose Method 1 when you're in a hurry or working with printed or textured bias that hides the topstitching. If you don't want topstitching on your bias, Method 2 is the best choice. Polar Fleece and boiled wool are so plush that it's best to use Method 3 for these fabrics.

Method 1

1. Set your machine for a straight stitch. Load it with matching thread, and then install an edge stitch presser foot.

2. Start stitching in the center of a pinned strip. Edge stitch as close as possible to all of the edges. As you approach the ends, use a stiletto to push under the raw edges. This gives you more control because you can fit a stiletto under a presser foot where your fingers can't safely reach. If the end of a strip stops at a seam, extend the end into the seam allowance instead of turning it under. Pivot at each corner.

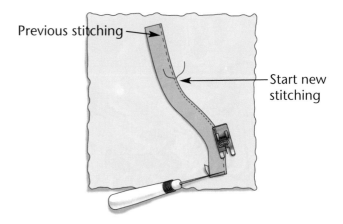

Previous stitching

Start new stitching

3. Attach the remaining strips in the same manner by following Step 2, above.

Method 2

1. Set your machine for a blind hem stitch with a short stitch length and narrow stitch width. Load the needle with matching or invisible thread, and install an edge stitch or zipper presser foot.

2. Start stitching in the center of a pinned strip. Edge stitch around all edges of each strip, positioning the work so that the left swing of the needle (the "zig") catches the edge of the strip and the straight portion of the stitch (the right swing) is on the garment, close to the edge of the strip. You begin this edge-stitching process by making the first stitch by turning the fly wheel by hand to ensure the needle clears the foot and enters the fabric at the desired lo-

cation. Stop with the needle down before reaching the first end.

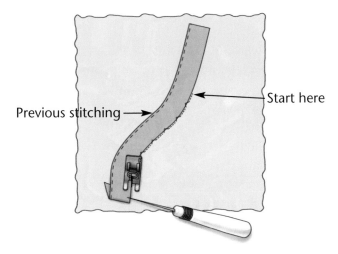

Previous stitching ——→

←—— Start here

3. As you approach the ends, use a stiletto to push under the raw edges. This gives you more control because you can fit a stiletto under a presser foot where your fingers can't safely reach. If the end of a strip stops at a seam, extend the end into the seam allowance instead of turning it under. Pivot at each corner.

FAQ FREQUENTLY ASKED QUESTION

How is a corner turned when working with a blind hem or a zigzag stitch?

As you approach the end of one side, stop exactly at the corner. Make sure that the needle is down in the fabric. At the corner, the needle should be on the right swing of the stitch. In other words, the very last stitch before the corner created the left "side" of the stitch. With the blind hem, mind you, the last stitch before the corner can also be straight, since the pattern is four straight stitches and then a zigzag. If it appears that the needle won't land at the corner, shorten or lengthen the stitch so that it's in the correct position.

Method 3

1. Thread your machine with matching or invisible thread. Use a transparent zigzag or an open-toe embroidery presser foot for better visibility when you stitch along the edges in the following steps for this process, Method 3.

2. Set the machine for a narrow zigzag (2 mm length and width) so that the left swing of the needle is on the fabric strip, while the right swing is just barely off the strip and on to the garment. If necessary, adjust the stitch to make it invisible when it is in position along the edge of the single fold or tubes.

3. Working with single fold or tubes, start stitching in the center of a pinned strip. Edge stitch around all sides of each strip. Stop with the needle down before reaching the first end.

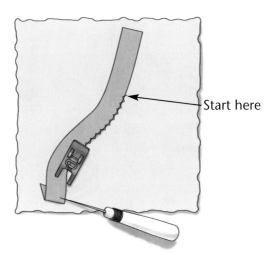

←—— Start here

4. As you approach the end, you need to hold it in position so it doesn't slip while you're stitching. Don't use a straight pin because it might be hit by the sewing machine needle. Instead, use a stiletto to hold down the raw edges. You don't have to turn under the raw ends. Simply stitch directly on the clean cut ends, because the fabric won't ravel. If the end of a strip stops at a seam, extend the end into the seam allowance. Pivot at each corner.

Product Information

Soon after I started teaching I realized that some sewing enthusiasts don't have easy access to supplies. They were so frustrated that I started selling products when I taught at consumer shows.

I can't emphasize enough that it's best to purchase supplies locally, if the products are available. Support the people who can help you every day. Thank them for being there, because many areas do not have great local shops.

For those of you who can't buy locally, check your favorite mail order catalog or order from my company, L.J. Designs.

L.J. Designs Patterns

(⌂4X-Available to size 4X)

879	Annapolis ⌂4X	798	Outback Jacket
723	Asymmetrical Tunic & Skirt ⌂4X	791	Sassy Jacket
897	Big Shirt Collection ⌂4X	847	Shanley Dress ⌂4X
867	Convertible Jacket ⌂4X	837	Shelby Jacket ⌂4X
777	Freedom Wrap	784	SophistiCoat
871	Galleria Jacket ⌂4X	117	Twister Scarf ⌂4X
875	Kanisha Collection ⌂4X	717	Ultimate Broomstick Skirt
887	Kinsey ⌂4X	773	Versa Jacket
877	LaConner Jackets ⌂4X	745	WOW! Tunic
766	Lyla's Vest	799	Zea Vest Collection ⌂4X
857	Nola Jumpers ⌂4X		

Design Plus Products

Design Plus Fusible Stay Tapes
(available in white or black)
 Straight
 Bias
 Super Fine Bias
 Super Fine Straight

Design Plus Stitch Through Elastic
Design Plus Ultra Soft Double Sided Web
Design Plus Water Soluble Paper
Sew Toasties Socks

Lyla's Helpers

Clover Bias Tape Maker
Clover Stiletto
Mini Iron
Perfect Pleater Board
Quill Stiletto
Stitch 'n Stretch Elastic
Sulky KK 2000

Threads

Elastic Thread
Fusible Thread
Glitter Thread
Halo Thread
Success Serger Yarn
Water Soluble Thread
Wonder Transparent Thread

Availability of patterns and products changes continually. To see the most current product offerings, visit Lyla's web site, call, or write for a current brochure.

L.J. Designs
P.O. Box 18923
Reno, NV 89511-0863

Phone 775-853-2207

or toll free 1-866-853-2207

www.LJDesignsOnline.com

L.J. Designs